"The whole forest, at least in Rock Creek hollow,
is simply rotting on the stump and falling....
We're losing 100 million years of evolution in less
than a hundred....This is a tragedy."

John Flynn

Fallen tulip poplar trees, Barrett's property, Coal River, West Virginia

Electric towers, Nitro, West Virginia

Dead red spruce and Fraser fir, road to Clingmans Dome, Great Smoky Mountains National Park, Tennessee

Predawn at a chemical plant in Decatur, Alabama

Tree trunk snap in the mixed mesophytic forest, Cold Springs Natural Area, Alabama

Steel plant stacks, Weirton, West Virginia

Dead trees on the summit, Mt. Mitchell, North Carolina

Stack and cooling tower at an electrical plant, near Nitro, West Virginia

Fraser fir along the Blue Ridge Parkway, North Carolina

AN
APPALACHIAN
TRAGEDY

APPALA

AN CHIAN TRAGEDY

AIR POLLUTION AND TREE DEATH

IN THE EASTERN FORESTS

OF NORTH AMERICA

Edited by Harvard Ayers, Jenny Hager, and Charles E. Little. Photographs by Jenny Hager

SIERRA CLUB BOOKS   SAN FRANCISCO

The Sierra Club, founded in 1892 by John Muir, has devoted itself to the study and protection of the earth's scenic and ecological resources—mountains, wetlands, woodlands, wild shores and rivers, deserts and plains. The publishing program of the Sierra Club offers books to the public as a nonprofit educational service in the hope that they may enlarge the public's understanding of the Club's basic concerns. The point of view expressed in each book, however, does not necessarily represent that of the Club. The Sierra Club has some sixty chapters coast to coast, in Canada, Hawaii, and Alaska. For information about how you may participate in its programs to preserve wilderness and the quality of life, please address inquiries to Sierra Club, 85 Second Street, San Francisco, CA 94105.

www.sierraclub.org/books

An Appalachian Tragedy

Editors	Harvard Ayers
	Jenny Hager
	Charles E. Little
Photographer	Jenny Hager
Design	Tom Suzuki
Chapter Text	Charles E. Little
Essayists	Chris Bolgiano
	Mary Hufford
	Orie L. Loucks
	Philip Shabecoff
	T. H. Watkins
Bibliography	William B. Grant
Index	Deborah E. Patton
Research	Carollyne Hutter
Copy Editor	Ruth B. Haas
Editorial Assistant	Janice M. Fowler

. . . .

Director of Design & Production, Sierra Club Books   Susan Ristow and David Charlsen

Project Editor, Sierra Club Books   Jim Cohee

Library of Congress Cataloging in Publication Data
An Appalachian tragedy:air pollution and tree death in the eastern forests of North America/edited by Harvard Ayers, Jenny Hager, and Charles E. Little; photographs by Jenny Hager
    p. cm.
    Includes bibliographical references and index.
    ISBN 0-87156-976-0 (cloth: alk. paper)
    1. Trees—Effect of air pollution on Appalachian Mountains. 2. Forest declines—Appalachian Mountains. 3. Forest ecology—Appalachian Mountains. 4. Air—Pollution—Environmental aspects—Appalachian Mountains. 5. Trees—Effect of air pollution on Appalachian Mountains—Pictorial works. 6. Forest declines—Appalachian Mountains—Pictorial works. 7. Forest ecology—Appalachian Mountains—Pictorial works. 8. Air—Pollution—Environmental aspects—Appalachian Mountains—Pictorial works.
I. Ayers, Harvard. II. Hager, Jenny. III. Little, Charles E.
SB745.A67 1998
577.3'27'0974—dc21
                                        97-34038
                                         CIP

Printed in Hong Kong

10 9 8 7 6 5 4 3 2 1

CONTENTS

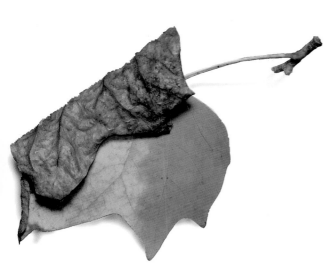

John Flynn
(1939–1996)

was a courageous writer and as moral

a man as we have ever known.

He loved his mountains and his neighbors,

and fought ceaselessly against those who

would take advantage of them.

This book is dedicated to his memory.

The Cry of the Mountains

A Foreword by Harvard Ayers

The frontispiece of this book contains a quotation from the late John Flynn, a friend and coworker. The word he uses—tragedy—may seem too strong to some, but it is absolutely accurate.

In fact, the tree death and forest decline that is the end result of 40 years of unremitting air pollution may be found throughout the Appalachian Mountains, not just in Flynn's beloved West Virginia. The impacts are manifested in varying degrees and with varying symptomatologies, but we now know from the work of our most respected forest ecologists that a pattern of death and decline extends all along the Appalachian chain from Maine to Georgia. The trees are dying: on the plateaus and ridges and crests, in the hollows and coves and river valleys, and at every elevation and at every latitude. The last stand of the once-magnificent eastern forest of North America is on its last legs.

And yet, as John Flynn also remarked after 20 years of reporting on the effects of pollution on this forest, "the story is a hard one to tell." What he really meant of course was not that the story is hard to tell, but that it is hard to get people to listen and to understand. No one wants to hear that an ecosystem crash this massive is imminent, indeed is under way in many areas. Public perception lags behind reality because the reality is unbearable.

And so the idea behind this publication, which we call *An Appalachian Tragedy* out of deference to John Flynn, is to take the reader on a kind of field trip, just as he did for many of us. Through photographs and text passages, and essays that explain and complement the photographs, we hope to bring the message home in such a way that the tragedy cannot be denied, shrugged off, or conveniently dismissed as environmental alarmism.

In my home forests of the Blue Ridge Mountains, for example, virtually all the trees, not just some of them, are in trouble at the mid- and high elevations. Indeed, my involvement in this book is mostly driven by my concern and downright sadness at losing my friends the sugar maples, the red spruce, the yellow birch, the Fraser fir, the beech, the

Newfound Gap, Great Smoky Mountains National Park, North Carolina

1

yellow buckeye, and perhaps my favorite, the mountain ash. From the vantage point of an airplane, I have seen patches of mountain hardwoods standing dead over tens and even hundreds of acres.

Hikes on Grandfather Mountain, Mt. Rogers, and Roan Mountain tell the same story—essentially all forests in the region above 4,500 feet are in deep trouble. Century after century, these forests have survived the ravages of bugs, diseases, harsh climate, and even rapacious human logging. Occasionally, single species have declined, or in one case, the chestnut, disappeared (due to a blight introduced nearly 100 years ago). But never have we witnessed the decline and mass death of almost all the major tree species of entire ecosystems.

For three decades now, pioneering scientists such as Gene Likens, Herbert Bormann, Hubert Vogelmann, Robert Bruck, Rick Webb, and Orie Loucks, to name a few, have been speaking out about the impact of air pollution on the eastern forests. They have told us that acid deposition (through rain, fog, snow, and dry particles), ground-level ozone, and other air pollutants have been taking their toll on nature.

Sugar maple dieback

Yet government studies, especially those conducted by scientists funded by industry, have denied that air pollution is a cause. Many even deny there is a problem at all. I have witnessed this denial firsthand in my dealings with the U.S. Forest Service, most vividly after I discovered whole ridges and hillsides of dying mountain hardwoods in a wilderness area in the Blue Ridge Mountains. I alerted the Forest Service about what I had seen, and they sent a staff biologist to investigate. His written report indicated that although he had looked at the same area I had, he found no unusual forest death. A week later, the biologist and I hiked into the area together. He was amazed when I showed him the hundreds of dead and dying sugar maples, yellow birch, and beech trees. He had literally walked right through a forest of dead trees and had not seen them. But then, in speaking with him about it, it was I who was amazed when he assured me that air pollution was not the culprit. He made that statement even though he was aware that a nearby air pollution monitor had measured dangerously high levels of tree-killing pollutants.

Actually, such clear evidence of denial can be found at all levels of the Forest Service. When permits were issued for me to conduct research meant to determine the extent and severity of forest decline and tree death near my home, top Forest Service officials made statements which indicated to me that they were totally unaware of the damage we were seeing on national forest lands. These are, mind you, lands that this federal agency is charged with protecting.

Denial has likewise been frequent among certain elements of the scientific community. The pioneering researchers mentioned above have endured a barrage of criticism from the old-line forest-science establishment, which tends to operate in lockstep with the Forest

Service and those political and economic entities whose interests this government agency has traditionally supported. While Loucks, Likens, Bruck, and others are well aware that proof of air pollution's role cannot be shown in absolute terms (in the same sense that smoking cannot be absolutely proven as the cause of lung cancer), they have been unafraid to assert that air pollution is fundamentally implicated in the unprecedented levels of tree death and decline in eastern forests over the past quarter-century. However, no good deed goes unpunished. For their honesty, they have had to pay the price in attacks on their credibility and in lost federal funding. Instead, they should be recognized for the scientific heroes they truly are.

Let me turn now to my fellow editors on this project and some of the others who have contributed substantially to it.

To begin with, it will be clear to all who even casually page through the book that in Jenny Hager we have a photographer of the first rank, whether the subject is a leaf, a forest, or a factory smokestack. While Jenny's photographs have appeared in many books, magazines, exhibits, and calendars, *An Appalachian Tragedy* brings together the largest body of her work published so far. As a mountaineer she has photographed all over the world, from the Himalayas to the Alps to the high ranges of Alaska and the western United States. For the past 4 years she has specialized in trees, especially those in the Appalachian Mountains. The editor of Sierra Club Books recently referred to her as the premier tree photographer in the country.

Charles E. Little, the noted environmental writer, developed the organizational concept of *An Appalachian Tragedy*, wrote the chapter introductions and the "super captions" for each of the photographic spreads, and recruited the essay writers and manuscript researchers and editors. Charles, who has served as head of natural resource policy research at the Library of Congress and of his own Washington think-tank (the American Land Forum), is the author of eleven books. Among his recent works is the highly acclaimed *The Dying of the Trees* (now in Penguin paperback), a finalist for the 1996 *Los Angeles Times* Book Prize. Reviewers have called it the most important environmental book published since *Silent Spring*.

The distinguished essayists for the book (more complete biographies may be found in the appendix) include the historian T. H. Watkins, whose biography of Harold Ickes was a finalist for the National Book Award; ecologist Orie L. Loucks, the scientific hero mentioned earlier, who holds a chair in ecosystem studies at Miami University; Chris Bolgiano, a widely published nature writer; Mary Hufford of the American Folklife Center of the Library of Congress and an expert on Appalachian culture; and Philip Shabecoff, who was the environmental reporter at the *New York Times* for many years and is the author of important books on the environmental movement. William B. Grant, a physicist with the National Aeronautics and Space Administration, prepared the extremely useful comprehensive bibliography.

As editors, Jenny, Charles, and I have been fortunate to have prominent graphic designer Tom Suzuki in charge of putting this book together. Formerly the art director at Time-Life Books, Tom has had his own studio since 1982, where he has designed award-winning illustrated books for the Smithsonian, Abrams, the National Gallery of Art, and many, many others. He has been a member of the core faculty of Stanford University's professional publishing course since the inception of this program in 1977. We are grateful too to Susan Ristow, production manager, and to Jim Cohee, editor at Sierra Club Books; to Carollyne Hutter, our researcher; to Ruth B. Haas, copy editor; to Janice Fowler, editorial assistant; and to Tom Suzuki's staff—Hea-Ran Cho, Constance Dillman, Kristin Bernhart, Julienne Lambre, and Virginia Suzuki.

S adly missing from this list is John Flynn himself, whose unremitting effort to bring the story of the Appalachian forests to light provided the primary creative impulse for this book. As a top science writer with a national reputation, John Flynn unflinchingly chronicled the widespread impacts of acid rain on the eastern forest, perhaps the first to do so. But during the 1980s, as the frontal assault on environmental reform gained power, he was hounded out of jobs on metropolitan dailies from Detroit, Michigan, to Jackson, Mississippi, by managements fearful of losing advertising revenue from polluting industries. Returning home, he spent the last 6 years of his life, much of it in virtual poverty, defending the forests of his native West Virginia as a freelance writer and publicist for citizen action.

It was John's 1991 series, "The Falling Forest," in the Beckley (West Virginia) *Register-Herald*, that introduced many of us to the startling revelation that acid rain had not only devastated the high ridges of the Appalachians, especially in Vermont and North Carolina, but the presumably better-protected midelevation valleys, coves, and hollows of the Appalachian plateau. Here the trees were literally falling down, dead, their roots rotted or the trunks snapped off halfway up. The forest floor was littered with dead trees, as the frontispiece shows.

John Flynn

During this period, John worked ceaselessly to bring influential scientists, government officials, environmentalists, photographers, and writers (including the editors and other contributors to this book) to the West Virginia mountains to see for themselves. He was a founder of the Lucy Braun Association, a scientific organization (named for the pioneering botanist of the mixed mesophytic forest), and of the Appalachia Forest Action Project—a "citizen science" program he led under the aegis of a consortium of organizations, including the Lucy Braun Association, the Sierra Club, Appalachia Science in the Public Interest, and Trees for the Planet.

To advance these efforts, John felt that photographic documentation of the devastated forests was needed to tell the Appalachian tree death story, and started working with Jenny Hager in 1994 toward that end. In time, the concept for this book arose.

Finally, in late February 1996, John met with the working group for the book in Washington. He was clearly exhausted, for he had been busy organizing the annual Lucy Braun Association conference that was to take place in March. After meeting with us, he had dinner with Mary Hufford and her husband Steve Oakes (Mary's essay begins on page 146), then drove back in the bitter cold to West Virginia in his old Pontiac. A few days later we heard that he was in the hospital at Charleston, having suffered a massive heart attack. Two operations were performed, but he never regained consciousness. Life support was removed, and he died at noon on March 7. We were all utterly devastated, and we still are. We and the forest had lost a true friend.

And so this is John Flynn's book, produced because of him and for him. However, John was an activist as well as a reporter, so while the book is significant in itself, it is also part of a larger project. Even as this foreword is being written, the Sierra Club's Southern Appalachian Eco-region program is conducting scientific research and planning a major public education campaign on Appalachian air pollution. The research will determine the extent and severity of tree death and forest decline in the high mountains of Virginia, Tennessee, and North Carolina. The educational campaign will ensure the distribution of *An Appalachian Tragedy* to decision-makers and the general public by means of a multi-media slide show presented across the entire region, from Maine to Georgia, as well as in parts of the Middle West, where much of the pollution comes from. This program, and the book itself, has been funded in significant part by the family of Harry Dalton. Harry is the founder of the Sierra Club's Appalachian Ecoregion Task Force. The text of our appreciation may be found at the end of the book.

In the end of course what really counts in this democratic country of ours is not grants or books or slide shows, but the people. If our Appalachian forests are to be saved, it will be because we the people have insisted on it. It is therefore our fervent hope as we send this volume off that the people who read it will understand this. That they will act in all the imaginative and resourceful ways Americans do when confronted with a national emergency. For those who do not think that the waning forests of the Appalachians may be a national emergency, I urge you to read on.

Boone, North Carolina
September 1997

Along the Spine of Time

These are our most ancient mountains, rising at the Gaspé Peninsula of Canada and running southward clear to Alabama, a distance of about 2,600 miles. In the U.S. part of the chain, the famed Appalachian Trail, conceived in 1921 by regional planner Benton MacKaye and completed in 1937, begins at Mt. Katahdin, Maine, and rambles for more than 2,000 miles southward to Springer Mountain, Georgia. For the most part, the trail keeps to the ridges along what writer Harry Middleton has called "the spine of time."

On the wooded slopes, along the ridges, and in the valleys of the Appalachians today are what remains of the Great American Forest, an unbroken blanket of giant trees once covering a third of our continental nation. Before the white man came, they say, a squirrel could run from the Atlantic shore clear to the Mississippi without once touching the ground. Such a squirrel would cruise through giant white pines 230 feet tall which the British would use for ship masts; over the top branches of black oaks 8 feet through the middle whose lowest branches were 50 feet above the ground; through chestnuts—half the forest cover in some places before the blight took them—whose limb spreads could be hundreds of feet wide with trunks 12 feet in diameter. Before the squirrel would come to rest, he would (if he took the scenic route) have scrambled across the leaves and branches of 200 different tree species, low and high, in a number of different forest types: white-red-jack pine, spruce-fir, oak-pine, oak-hickory, maple-beech-birch, among others. If his east–west excursion were at about the middle of the chain, he would start at sea level on the coastal plain of North Carolina, rising through the piedmont laced with muddy rivers, to the summit of the highest Appalachian peak, Mt. Mitchell. Pausing there, he could see the daunting serrated ridges stretching seemingly to infinity, disappearing into the blue haze that is characteristic of this part of the range. A thoughtful squirrel might give up at that point and return to the lowlands.

Indeed, the Appalachians were seen as a barrier for the earliest white settlers, who for 200 years after their arrival in the late sixteenth century

Appalachian Mountain ridges at dawn, from a viewpoint in Roan Mountain State Park, North Carolina

clung close to the shore, cultivating first the river bottoms, then the thin-soiled slopes of the piedmont, which they mercilessly logged off. It was not until about 1800 that there was a serious trans-Appalachian migration to the West. And so, having logged off the piedmont on the east side, they logged off the western slopes along the rivers flowing to the Mississippi. By the mid-1800s, some 7,000 square miles a year were being cleared.

What remained were the mountains, seemingly eternal in the rocky steeps, wooded coves, and alpine meadows. That they are not eternal in the face of the assaults of airborne pollution is what this book will deal with in later sections, but for now it is well to celebrate this magnificent remnant of the Great Eastern Forest, not only in its natural diversity, but in its cultural diversity too. For as the migrants moved across the mountains from the earliest times, they left the marks of their lives there—post-and-rail fences, farmhouses, barns, corncribs, springhouses, churches.

The images and words you encounter in this section, and in Tom Watkins' wonderful essay which concludes it, are good ones to keep in mind as you go through the rest of the book, for here we intend to praise the mountains. Surely, we must never forget that no matter what difficulties beset the Appalachians, they are still beautiful, still filled with spirit and with life.

Roaring Fork Creek, Great Smoky Mountains National Park, Tennessee

Green ferns and groundcover, Gregory Ridge, Great Smoky Mountains
National Park, Tennessee

Right, wet sugar maple leaves, autumn, Moraine State Park,
Pennsylvania

Far right, mushrooms, rock, and green moss,
Shenandoah National Park, Virginia

The Foundation of the Forest

It is the forest soils that sustain the forest, soils that are in turn created over centuries by the forest itself in a cycle of small miracles. Roots and lichens break down the rocks into finer and finer material. The groundcovers keep the surface of the soil moist, aiding decomposition, which adds nutrients; mushrooms feed on decomposed woody materials beneath, decomposing them further; while lichens and moss on a tree trunk provide food for wild animals. When walking through an Appalachian forest, one's gaze is mostly upward, but where the forest begins is at one's feet. Here the view is equally fascinating for it shows the ecological intricacy of a forest as a whole community.

Tree trunk with lichen and moss, Mt. Mitchell State Park, North Carolina

Springtime in the Garden of the Appalachians

Facing page, wild red azaleas on Gregory Bald, Great Smoky Mountains National Park, Tennessee

Above the brilliant small wildflowers of the forest floor, such as the trilliums and violets, azaleas and rhododendrons, some almost tree-like, have always made the mountains vivid in the spring. One of the azaleas, the rare Rhodora, growing in the New England Appalachians, moved Ralph Waldo Emerson to create what many think is his finest poem.

The Rhodora:
On Being Asked, Whence Is the Flower?

In May, when sea-winds pierced our solitudes,
I found the fresh Rhodora in the woods,
Spreading its leafless blooms in a damp nook,
To please the desert and the sluggish brook.
The purple petals, fallen in the pool,
Made the black water with their beauty gay;
Here might the red-bird come his plumes to cool,
and court the flower that cheapens his array.
Rhodora! if the sages ask thee why
This charm is wasted on the earth and sky,
Tell them, dear, that if eyes were made for seeing,
Why thou wert there, O rival of the rose!
I never thought to ask, I never knew;
But, in my simple ignorance, suppose
the self-same Power that brought me there
             brought you.

Top and middle, large-flowered trillium and wild yellow violet, Great Smoky Mountains National Park

Left, wild pink Catawba rhododendron on Roan Mountain, Pisgah National Forest, North Carolina

Moose, Baxter State Park, Maine

Bald eagle, Grandfather Mountain, North Carolina

Creatures of the Forest

An astonishing range of animals and birds—the species most of us seek out to tell our friends what we have seen—depend on the forests of the Appalachians, the place they have called home since long before human-kind even dreamed of these mountains. Beyond those shown here on this page are wild turkey, deer, bear, grouse, fox, otter, wolves, weasels, hawks, cottontails, and hundreds more birds and mammals that dine in the forests and are sometimes dined upon.

Wolves and bears command the most attention, of course. The red wolf, previously extinct in the wild, is being reintroduced into the southern Appalachians with some success. This species, smaller than the gray wolf, looks and acts much like the coyote, with which it is often confused. The black bear of the Appalachians is unmistakable. Less aggressive than the grizzly, black bears nevertheless can be dangerous if they become "addicted" to human food.

Top, common loon and (*middle*) pileated woodpecker, Cades Cove, Great Smoky Mountains National Park, Tennessee

Gray fox

Redbuds and dogwoods, Coal River, West Virginia

Trees covered with rime ice and frost, Clingmans Road, Great
Smoky Mountains National Park, Tennessee

To Every Season There Is a Forest

When we go to the woods, it is not a single place we go to, but different places at different times of the year. The forest constantly changes and at every season presents us with a new image of itself in which different trees are prominent at different times.

In springtime we notice the flowering trees. Some, like the dogwood, the sarvis bush, and redbud, are quite small but because of their vivid colors are seemingly the most present. In summer the leafiest of the deciduous trees, such as the tulip poplar with its heavy green foliage, dominates the scene, shading the forest floor in competition with its neighbors. And in autumn particular deciduous trees command our attention—the maples, the beech, and the oaks in an array of oranges, yellows, and reds.

Once the leaves are gone in winter, we see more than at any other time how the forest is composed. The trees become individuals, distinct in our sight, not part of a mass of foliage clamoring for our attention. The woods are still, standing quietly, at rest before the cycle begins again.

Top, autumn leaves at Falling Water, Pennsylvania

Middle, bare trees along Newfound Gap Road, Great Smoky Mountains National Park, North Carolina

Bottom, tulip poplars, Great Smoky Mountains National Park, Tennessee

Horses grazing at Cades Cove, Great Smoky Mountains National Park, Tennessee

First Families

Most of the Indians are gone, though a few Cherokees remain in the mountains of North Carolina. But they left their signature on the land and on the trees. The pasture at left reminds us that when the white settlers arrived, "old fields" for pasturing and crops had already been made for them. These were clearings in the forest where Indians grew corn and native beans, *uppowoc* (tobacco), pumpkins, gourds, and squash.

The bent tree below, in Bankhead, Alabama, is a type of historical marker—of the battle between the Creek and the Chickasaw Indians in the late 1700s. Normally, marker trees such as this were bent in one direction—by twisting the stem when the tree was small to mark a turn in the trail. This one was created with a double bend in two opposite stems to commemorate the battle.

The "arborglyph" is also an historical marker. In the 1830s, the Cherokees were forced by the U.S. government to leave the mountains, along a route called "The Trail of Tears." Those who escaped the banishment fled to the mountains and carved their tribal symbol on this beech tree—a birdman with a high-crowned hat.

Left, "marker" tree, Bankhead National Forest, Alabama

Right, an arborglyph at Brushy Creek, Bankhead National Forest

Mountain Pioneers

It could be said that homesteading started here. The seaboard lowlands were taken up by plantation owners, and the less desirable piedmont lands filled with sidehill farms that quickly depleted the thin soils. Only the

Post-and-rail fence, Humpback Rocks Pioneer Exhibition, Blue Ridge Parkway, Virginia

mountains were left for those brave enough to enter their fastnesses and carve a living from the forests. The Scots-Irish, predominately, came in and in many cases stayed in, creating an indigenous culture all their own.

Jefferson, himself a mountain farmer in Virginia, though of gentler and more capacious lands than those shown on this page, admired the gumption of these early settlers. It was his thought that every American family

should have its little plot of land to farm, just as the small plots were farmed in the mountains. "It is not too soon," Jefferson wrote from France to a friend in Virginia in 1785, "to provide by every possible means that as few as possible shall be without a little portion of land. The small landholders are the most precious part of the state."

Jefferson's dream would not be realized until the Homesteading Act of 1862, and the land distribution that followed helped to settle the nation from coast to coast as the Appalachians were breached, the Mississippi crossed, and the great billion-acre heartland turned to agriculture. But it was the mountain people—mostly left behind in the remarkable Westering—who provided the model in the small homesteads of the Appalachians.

Top, farmstead cornfields, Oconaluftee, North Carolina

Above, at Tipton's Homestead, Great Smoky Mountains National Park, Tennessee

Cabins and Churches

The Scandinavians, Finns, and Swedes mainly, and the Germans coming in to the Pennsylvania mountains, taught the Scots-Irish and the English settlers how to clear the land of trees and build log cabins. This was a community enterprise, and the assembling of such structures was quickly completed—perhaps a matter of a day or two. The technique spread rapidly up and down the mountains. Later, the churches were built. Many of them appear to be frame structures, but underneath the smooth siding (easily obtainable after the sawmills arrived) may be walls of logs.

A log cabin and chicken coop, Humpback Rocks, Blue Ridge Parkway, Virginia

Methodist church at Cades Cove, Great Smoky Mountains National Park, Tennessee

Family Times...

Facing page, Wesley Scarbro and his young brother-in-law, Justin Walker squirrel hunting in a Rock Creek, West Virginia, hickory grove

A forest is a community made up of trees and animals and soils—all the different families that create an ecosystem. In the Appalachians, perhaps more than most mountains, the human family is an integral part of the ecosystem and has been ever since the first European settlers got together to build the first log cabin. In these mountains the skills and pleasures of forest life are not just artifacts celebrated in historical exhibits but are handed down from generation to generation. Also handed down are the lessons of life in the family-oriented culture of the mountains. In the hunt for a squirrel for a Brunswick stew, in the cracking of walnuts out the back door, in harvesting the ginseng roots with the special hoes made for the purpose come understandings of self-reliance, love and respect for nature and neighbor, and one's responsibility for the welfare of the community.

Left, Herman Williams cracking black walnuts with his grandson Nicholas, Clear Fork, West Virginia

Below, Carla Pettry, with her daughter Natalie and her mother, Shelby Estep, posing with "seng hoes," Horse Creek, West Virginia

... and Folkways

A musical get-together at a Beckley, West Virginia, flea market

In the mountains, a tailgate party is likely to produce an impromptu concert, not beer and burgers. Mountain music derives from early Scottish, Irish, and English sources, and it changes as the songs are passed along from musician to musician. There are a hundred versions of the centuries-old lament, "Barbara Allen," in the folk music archives of the Library of Congress. Appalachian folksong is not confined to the antique ballad, however. As much a part of the repertoire are contemporary themes of railroading, coal mining, logging, and the predatory nature of the corporate bosses, absentee landowners,

and politicians. Sometimes the songs are nonsense or elaborate jokes belted out just for the fun of it.

Also passed along are the rural arts of basket weaving and quilt-making. Both these activities, while originally undertaken for quite practical reasons, have in the Appalachians become high-level vernacular art forms. The quilt pattern here is called "Windmill." Others made by the group shown, who meet weekly, are "Grandmother's Flower Garden," "Log Cabin," "Hole in the Barn Door," "Hopscotch." News of the community is thoroughly analyzed at the quilting sessions, some of them lasting all day. Quilts are sold at the annual ramp supper to raise money for a community building known locally as "The Ramp House."

Top, Newt Washburn teaches his granddaughter how to make a brown ash basket, Bethlehem, New Hampshire

Above, quilting bee at Drew's Creek, West Virginia, with (*clockwise from left*) Mabel Brown, Jenny Bonds, Margie Miller, Nancy Jarrell, and Sadie Miller

Recreation and Inspiration

Facing page, backpacker at Green Falls, Baxter State Park, Maine

The Appalachians provide recreational opportunities within a day's drive or less for nearly two-thirds of the American population. Some 17 national forests are here. As for units of the national park system, Shenandoah, the Blue Ridge Parkway, and the Great Smoky Mountains are far and away the most popular in the nation, with visitation approaching 50 million a year when taken together.

The mountains also contain some 54 congressionally designated wilderness areas, including such treasures as Pemigewasset in Vermont, Dolly Sods in West Virginia, and Brasstown in Georgia. Every year some 175 hardy souls, give or take, hike the entire 2,144-mile Appalachian Trail, end to end.

Indeed, in these mountains recreation is not simply a matter of spending idle hours out of doors but can be an experience of nature that is rugged, rewarding, and inspirational.

Top, cross-country skiing at Meadows Track, Blueberry Hill, Goshen, Vermont

Left, canoeing in Kent Pond, Sherburne, Vermont

Below, trout fishing in the Toe River, North Carolina

Monitoring the Forest

Facing page, Ken Wills and Jody Schaub measure trees in Bankhead National Forest, Alabama. Wills *(below)* is forest ecologist for the Appalachian Forest Action Project

As later chapters will describe in some detail, the forests of Appalachia have been beset by air pollution and other human-caused stresses. Although the scientists of the U.S. Forest Service and other government agencies might be expected to keep tabs on forest health in the Appalachians, the fact is that their research, especially during the 1980s and early 1990s, was often politically influenced.

This failure persuaded a group of independent scientists and policy experts to appeal to the citizens of the Appalachians to help them undertake an unbiased effort to monitor the health of the forest. This they have done, with in fact the expert assistance of a number of newly responsive and ecologically oriented local Forest Service officials. Two hundred citizen-scientists, working with trained ecologists such as Ken Wills, pictured here, now monitor the health of trees on 158 sites in 5 states. The findings: tree mortality is at three to five times historical norms.

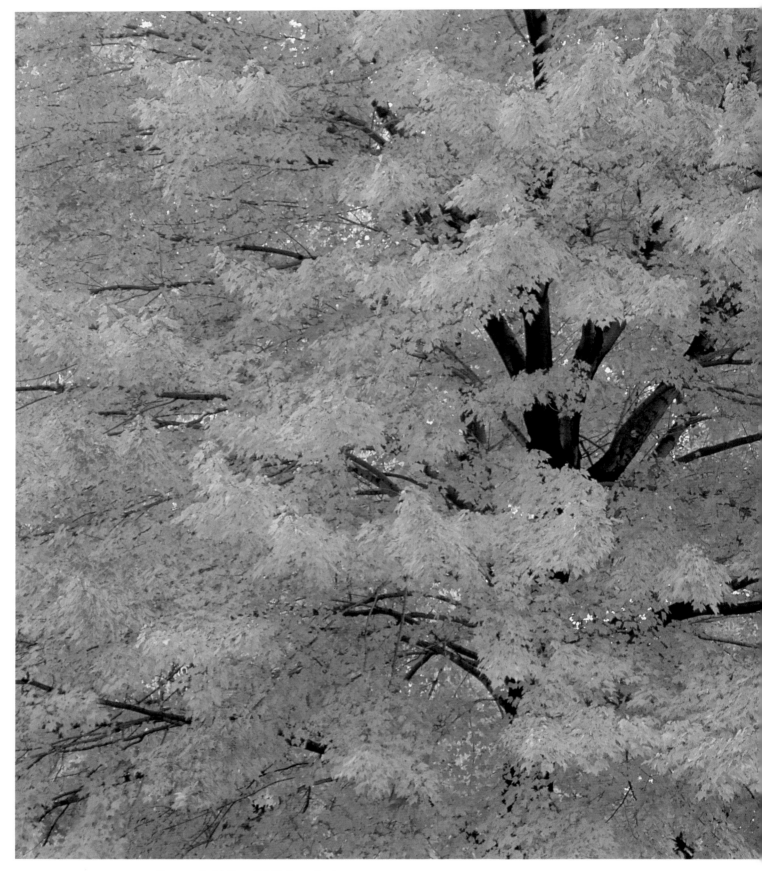

Sugar maple, McConnel's Mill, Pennsylvania

How Sweet It Is

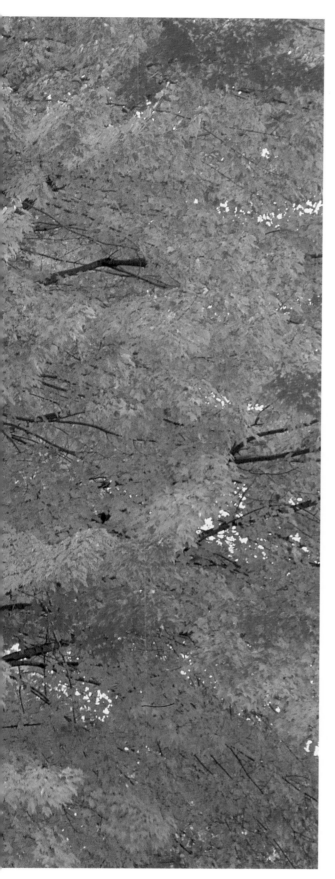

Maples are a symbol of the northern Appalachians, particularly the state of Vermont, though sugaring takes place in all of New England as well as New York, Pennsylvania, and Ohio. "Sugaring" is the term used for both sugar and syrup production. In fact, maple sugar was not surpassed by cane sugar as a household sweetener until 1875.

The useful maples have two other economic values. First, the extremely hard, durable, and yet easily worked wood is ideal for furniture, flooring, and even certain aircraft components. Second, the maples help localities cash in on tourism, now a major economic force. Every October, by plane, train, car, and bus, fall foliage lovers arrive by the millions to view the magnificent seasonal display in the mountains in which the maples have a starring role.

Top, sugar house in Pomfret, Vermont

Right, collecting maple sap in a Vermont sugarbush

Agriculture at the Human Scale

If in California, the Middle West, and the Great Plains agriculture has been turned into a mega-industry with thousand-acre spreads, massive machinery, and hefty payrolls, the farms of the Appalachians have, by virtue of the small spaces they occupy and the cultural values they embody, remained at the human scale.

Here farming is less commercial than it is cultural (even though some can make a whole living from it). The emphasis is on diversity of crops and livestock, on family labor, and on the local marketing of its products, such as the mason-jar display shown here. Even those who have no commercial aspirations whatsoever have their own garden plot. The canned goods are for household consumption and are given to friends and neighbors.

As for Vermont's cheese, it is still famous, even though most U.S. cheese production now takes place in the Middle West. The state has always tried to hang on to its mountain-style agriculture. In fact, the area that was to become the state of Vermont (the fourteenth in the Union) was once called the "breadbasket" to the colonies. When the wheat went west, Vermont became the dairying capital of the nation. However, the cows went west too, most of them. Yet the mountains endure, and the pastures are kept open, which gives the old Green Mountain State much of its charm.

Sunrise at Jenne Farm, South Woodstock, Vermont

Canned goods from the garden of Vivian and Bruce Jarrell, Dry Creek, West Virginia

Dewey Gunnoe, surveying his garden in Stickney, West Virginia

Bole

Take away the chainsaw, substitute a two-man saw or even a double-bitted axe, and this picture could accurately record an event taking place 200 years ago. A big tulip poplar has been felled, its bole and larger limbs to be cut into sawtimber, its branches into stove lengths for heating and cooking. When the trees are cut down selectively, the forest can endure. This is still possible on privately owned forest land, although sometimes a family strapped for cash will succumb to the blandishments of a logger promising them riches if he is allowed to clearcut. For the forest land of the Appalachians, which is mostly owned by huge multinational corporations eager to obtain immediate profits, the fate of magnificent boles like the one shown here might well be to wind up as a pile of chips for particle-board or paper products.

Danny Williams, selective cutting in Rock Creek, West Virginia

I Wonder as I Wander

In 1933, while visiting the southern Appalachians, the famed folksong authority John Jacob Niles collected a unique ballad—one he said he had never heard before, nor could later trace to European sources. (Some believe he may have at least partially composed the music himself.) The ballad was given to him by a young woman named Annie Morgan in Murphy, North Carolina. Despite the question about the music, these were her words:

> *I wonder as I wander out under the sky*
> *How Jesus our Saviour did come for to die*
> *For poor orn'ry people like you and like I . . .*
> *I wonder as I wander out under the sky.*

Now familiar, the hauntingly mysterious minor-key phrase, "I wonder as I wander out under the sky" is especially apt for the Appalachians today. For the fate of the mountains is in doubt, as shrouded as the old valleys and hollows and coves beneath the blanket of early morning fog, as the photograph suggests.

Everything is known about the Appalachians, at least thought to be known by the millions that frequent them. And yet nothing is known—neither their fragile ecosystems nor the enduring culture of their people. Such ignorance is a pity because as the following essay by historian Tom Watkins makes plain, of all places in our continental nation, these "round-shouldered old mountains" bespeak the essence of the American experience most evocatively.

Sunrise and fog, Newfound Gap Road, Great Smoky Mountains National Park, North Carolina

The View from Brasstown Bald

By T. H. Watkins

Peter Kirby is telling me about problems as we zip up US 19 from Atlanta on our way to Brasstown Bald in Chattahoochee National Forest, a federal land unit pocketed in northern Georgia (on the maps, the Chattahoochee looks as if it has oozed out of the bottom of South Carolina's Nantahala National Forest like a renegade amoeba). Kirby is director of The Wilderness Society's regional office in Atlanta and with his counterparts in the Sierra Club's Southern Appalachian Highlands Ecoregion Task Force and other local and national conservation groups has been fighting the good conservationist fight in the southern Appalachians for nearly 10 years. He knows more than he probably wants to know about the afflictions of overdevelopment, air and water pollution, and bad forest management, and speaks with the authoritative, rapid-fire articulation of someone who has talked about problems many, many times before to journalists, foresters, congressional committees, sundry citizens' groups, and anyone else who will listen—though his passion seems undiminished by all the repetition.

This first leg of our journey is pretty dismal, with developmental blurs that smudge the view on both sides of the highway, one housing development after another, one strip mall after another—and in place after place where nothing yet stands, the fresh red scars of road-building and site clearance tell you that something soon enough will be built, a cinéplex here, a condominium complex there, human dreams of enterprise rising lotuslike from the mud. When it rains, as it has been doing over the past several days this winter, the rivers run chocolate with eroded soil, as does the Chestatee River as we cross the bridge that spans it, the water below churning and twisting through its channel like a long brown snake.

But as we swing through the old gold mining town of Dahlonega, which manages to be historic without being quaint, the mountains themselves loom just ahead of us like a benediction, gray and indistinct in the misty morning light, their topmost edges feathered with leafless winter trees. Above us, a steady cold wind propels lumpy gray clouds past the rounded peaks, sometimes pushing at the clouds with such rude force that they are ripped into tatters, revealing patches of clear blue sky here and there before joining together and breaking apart again. We are soon deep into the national forest, grinding up the mountains along a two-lane road that curls around the shoulders of the old hills, past the occasional privately owned hollow—"hollers," they would be called by most of those who live in them—studded with ancient wooden farm buildings, rusty, paint-scabbed trailer-homes, and the long ugly sheds of chicken farms, past steep road cuts thick with

Appalachian sunrise, Roan
Mountain State Park,
North Carolina

dark-leaved rhododendron and mountain laurel—both just "ivy" to the local folk, who do not make too much of a distinction between the two species. And then the private inholdings are gone entirely and on both sides of us there is only forest, dark and tangled and deceptively primeval, steeper slopes laced everywhere by high thin waterfalls that tumble down through thickets of ivy and over the faces of slick black rocks. I know that the forest I see is only a few human generations old, most of the original old growth of the mountains having been stripped away by loggers over the course of the past century, but it does not matter. Whatever its precise age, this is definitive forest, and it takes no great stretch of the mind to picture it thick with bears and deer and wild turkeys and the shadowy stealth of Indians and white people out to murder one another. Trees everywhere, black oaks, red oaks, and white oaks; eastern white pine and flowering dogwood; yellow poplars and eastern hemlocks; shagbark hickory, maple, spruce, beech, and birch. These and other species mix with their understory growth to create a vegetative porridge that spreads up the slopes, is interrupted briefly by the exposed granite face of Blood Mountain towering ahead of us, then spills its rich diversity of life over the ridges and into unseen coves and along big and little creeks chattering their way down the mountains.

We stop for a quick lunch of sandwiches at some picnic tables outside an outfitter's store at Neels Gap, where the Appalachian Trail comes

down from Levelland Mountain to the north, crosses the highway, then heads back up to Blood Mountain to the south. Kirby gives some overnight camping advice to a pair of young backpackers who have come in off the trail, then we return to the car and resume our trip, worrying about the overcast, which we fear may make it impossible to see much once we reach the top of Brasstown Bald, at 4,784 feet the highest point in Georgia.

We need not have concerned ourselves. The same wind that bends our eyebrows and rattles our clothes as we leave Kirby's car at the parking lot and hike up the steep seven or eight hundred feet to the Brasstown Bald visitor center, has ripped most of the clouds from the sky. The center is closed for the winter season, but from its huge wood-beam platform we are given a 360-degree view of the southern Appalachians, and even though Kirby keeps telling me that what lies before me is not everything I could see on a really clear day, it is more than enough to give me a feeling for these mountains I probably could not have experienced in any other way.

There is, above all, a sense of bigness here that surprises me. These are not, after all, the Rockies or the Sierra Nevada, with their towering crags and snow-choked divides, and I was expecting to find the Appalachians disappointing once I had the chance to look out over them. I am definitely not disappointed. They are genuinely awesome, these round-shouldered old mountains, and I am transfixed as Kirby guides my gaze through the compass, all talk of problems forgotten now in the sheer joy he finds in revealing this spread of much-loved landscape. To the east is the "swag" of the Blue Ridge, he says, a long undulating wave of stone and forest beyond which lies the piedmont region, sloping down to the coastal plain, then to the edge of the continent and the Atlantic Ocean. To the south southwest is the arc of peaks and ranges through which we have just driven, and somewhere in the distance I know that the unseen southernmost spur of the entire Appalachian chain would be poking into the middle of the northeastern quadrant of Alabama. To the west northwest, the mountains fall into Tennessee and the Appalachian Plateau in descending parallel ridges.

All of this has its fascination, but it is the mountains to the north northeast that hold my gaze the longest, for it is in this misty jumble of ridges and peaks stretching to the farthest horizon that I begin to understand the geographic eminence of a landform that curves 2,000 miles in length, that separates one physiographic province from another down most of that long curve, that has dictated the course of rivers, evolved complex and diverse ecotones, and determined the fate of human aspirations from archaic times to the street accident called the twentieth century. And something else: it is from my perch here on the highest point in Georgia, looking north toward the Smokies and the unseen ranges beyond, with the wind in my ears and my eyes full of mountains, that I gain the fullest sense of the terrible splendid wildness that still defines the Appalachians from the bottom to the top, the whole two thousand miles of it clear to the Canadian border and beyond.

It is not a "pure" wildness, I suppose; humans have been at work here too long and too variously for much uncorrupted nature to remain. But it is wildness nevertheless, a generally intact sweep of landscape where the protocols of nonhuman nature still prevail, where the sweet loneliness of solitude may still be earned, where connections to the living world around you can still be found and nurtured, where one of David Brower's most trenchant remarks still finds validation. "The wild places are where we began," he said. "When they end, so do we."

"You know," Kirby says, "whenever I drive up into these mountains and leave all the civilization of the flatland behind, I feel that I am coming home."

Yes.

As a geographic entity, the Appalachian Mountains are a lesson in the earth's violence and distressing instability. Back during a stretch of time so old that human attempts to understand it are ludicrous, the planet's semiliquid outer layer supported a collection of oceanic and continental plates made up of lighter stuff that floated here and there like huge ice floes according to the dictates of planetary convection, crunching into one another, grinding against one another, splitting apart, joining together, forming great seas, then closing them off. About 500 million years ago, one such plate, now dubbed Laurentia, comprising much of what is now North America, Greenland, and the British Isles, was slammed into by another plate, called Baltica, comprising much of what is now northern Europe. Baltica slid under Laurentia with such force that it gave birth to a series of volcanic peaks in what geologists describe as the Taconian Orogeny. This was followed a hundred million years or so later by the Arcadian Orogeny, during which continued crunching between the two plates drove up another

range (the original volcanic peaks had long since eroded, their grains carried away and deposited to become various sedimentary layers). These new peaks were called the Caledonide Mountains and occupied both sides of the collision point. Then the masses began tearing apart, the eastern section of the Caledonides drifting east across the great trench that would become the Atlantic Ocean, while on Laurentia primitive forms of plant and animal life—insects, arthropods, amphibians, giant ferns, horsetails, and club mosses—were buried under layers of sediment washing down from the eroding mountains, compressed, heated, and ultimately turned into coal.

Over the next couple of hundred million years, all of the earth's plates joined to form two great masses of floating crust, the one in the north called the Old Red Sandstone Continent, that in the south, Godwanaland. Inexorably, these two drifted toward one another and finally collided, producing the last of the Appalachians' mountain-building episodes, the Alleghenian Orogeny, which shoved up the ancient, complex mix of igneous, metamorphic, and sedimentary rock that had been assembled over the preceding eons—the granites and quartzites, sandstones, limestones, shales, and dolomites—creating long wrinkles and ridges and plateaus and lumpy agglomerations of mountain morphology in a swath that embraced portions of Newfoundland, Quebec, New Brunswick, Maine, Vermont, New Hampshire, New York, Pennsylvania, Ohio, West Virginia, Virginia, North Carolina, South Carolina, Kentucky, Tennessee, Georgia, and Alabama. Probably no other mountain range in the world is shared by so many political entities.

For millions of years, the two great plates whose collision had raised up the ancestral Appalachians stuck together as one big place, called Pangaea. But this crustal marriage, too, was doomed. About 200 million years ago, the new continent split apart, one portion drifting vaguely southeast and evolving into the various parts of what would become Europe, Africa, and Asia, the rest drifting vaguely northwest and reassembling itself into what is now Greenland, Nova Scotia, North America, and South America. The continental divorce was generally final by about 100 million years ago, though it should be noted that the continental plates are still drifting away from one another. "Europe," Scott Weidensaul notes in his lovely *Mountains of the Heart* (from which much of my discussion of the Appalachians' geological history is taken), "already is fractionally farther from the Appalachians than it was when you started this chapter."

Then came the cycles of glaciation, when the cutting tool of ice scoured and shaped everything as far south as western Pennsylvania before retreating for the last time about 12,000 years ago. What was left behind, wrinkling the skin of the eastern third of the future United States of America, was not a single mountain range but many individual ranges, peaks, and ridge-and-valley-and-plateau complexes. At the northernmost end lay the Longfellow Mountains of Maine, with 5,268-foot Mt. Katahdin as the state's highest point, and at the southernmost end, the Talledega Mountains of Alabama, with 2,407-foot Cheaha Mountain as that state's greatest height of land. Between these two points were the White Mountains and the Presidential Range of New Hampshire; the Green Mountains of Vermont; the Poconos, Shawangunks, Catskills, and Taconic Hills of New York; the Allegheny Mountains of Pennsylvania; the Cheat Mountains of West Virginia; the Shenandoah Mountains of Virginia; the Black Mountains and Snowbird Mountains of North Carolina; and, as the two largest single geographic bodies in the entire chain, the Great Smoky Mountains of Tennessee–North Carolina and the Blue Ridge, whose swags and swales descended all the way from northwestern Virginia to the point at which I saw them from the visitor center at Brasstown Bald. (For the purposes of this book, the Appalachians' northern neighbors, the Adirondack Mountains in northeastern New York, also will come under discussion from time to time, although they are composed of rocks much older than those of the Appalachians: 600-million-year-old intrusions of what is called anorthosite—a rock also found on the moon—that were thrust up through the crust of the earth by subterranean forces independent of the various collisions of the continental plates; indeed, there are indications that the Adirondacks are still rising.)

Into all this geology time wrote a hundred rivers and countless creeks, each carrying out the eternal task of carrying the land to the sea, bit by minuscule bit. In the process, the water not only rounded off most of the sharp edges of the ancient peaks, but wore away old sedimentary deposits and exposed sunlit "coves" like Cades Cove in the Great Smoky Mountains, whose underlying rock is younger than the rock in the mountains that surround it; or deepened existing cracks and splits in the folded and faulted old rocks, like Linville Gorge in the Blue Ridge of North Carolina, where the Linville River tumbles beautifully 1,700 feet down through several hundred million years of geology; or helped shape lovely wide valleys, like that sculpted by the Shenandoah River curving gently between the Blue Ridge and the Shenandoah Mountains in northern Virginia. Everywhere, the water helped to shape the Appalachians into a convoluted mix of landforms more than matched by the extraordinary diversity of life that flourished on their mountaintops and slopes, in their coves and valleys and dark moist places.

Here were the bogs, sedge meadows, and tree-ridden jumble of mountains of the great northern forests of Maine, New Hampshire, and Vermont, whose open places were a minor riot of bladderwort and ragwort, bellflowers and marigolds, violets and pitcher plants, rose pogonias and fringed orchids. Along the edges of the open spaces at lower elevations sprouted a mix of alternate-leafed dogwood, black cherry, gray and paper birches, elderberry, Canada yew, eastern hemlock, balsam poplar, red and sugar maples, and several species of oak and pine—especially the elegant, towering white pines that once dominated a wide belt of America from Maine to Minnesota. Higher up the mountains were the needle-leafed spruce-fir forests—balsam firs and red and black spruce.

Many northern plant species extended below the region of the northern forest, and plant life of all kinds grew richer and more complex the farther south the mountains trended, until in the richly soiled, temperate, and well-watered forests of the Great Smokies and other

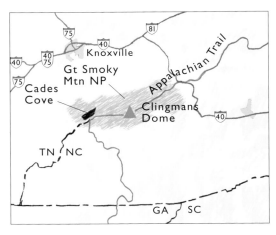

southern ranges they exploded into a startlingly fecund botanical mélange—some 2,500 species, including those in the then-dominant association of hickory-chestnut forests (before the great blight beginning at the turn of the century wiped out most of the chestnuts by the 1930s) and more than 100 additional species of trees and over 1,500 species of flowers, shrubs, mosses, and ferns. Nowhere was this fecundity more richly expressed than in the hardwood cove forests that could be found up to about 4,500 feet—ecotones that possessed yellow poplars and eastern hemlocks hundreds of years old and a couple of dozen feet in circumference, together with scores of such other species as blackgum, butternut, black walnut, black cherry, American beech, and white pine, and many species of oak. Below all these trees, down where the sunlight stabbed through the canopy in mote-speckled beams, the forest floor was lumpy with moss-covered decomposing logs above which grew long-branched flowering dogwood and eastern redbud, white ash and yellow buckeye, sourwood and slippery elm, and many species of magnolias. Thickets of rhododendron and mountain laurel were interspersed with maidenhair and hay-scented ferns, spicebush and wild geraniums, Carolina silverbell and highbush blueberry, while bright-green carpets of the ground cover called princess pine gleamed in the murky light.

Animal life was no less various, including some of the most impressive "megafauna" in the American lexicon. Throughout the Appalachians, black bears harvested grubs, berries, voles, mice, chipmunks, and woodrats, while wolves—gray (or timber) in the north, red in the south—panthers, red foxes, and even the occasional pair of coyotes made a good living from whitetailed deer, though in the north they could add moose and woodland caribou to their diets. River otters sported in the streams, fishing for spotfin chub and brook trout. Salamanders—34 species of salamanders, including the red-backed, pygmy, northern dusky, and Jefferson—squig-gled in the secret wet places, with wood turtles and leopard frogs as neighbors. Above, southern flying squirrels sailed from tree to tree and broad-winged hawks, red-tailed hawks, harriers, bald eagles, and golden eagles kept their eyes peeled for something furred or feathered they could scavenge or hunt, while most of the known species of owls cruised the woods and meadows of night. Red-cockaded and pileated

woodpeckers kept up a rapid rat-a-tat-tat of noise; tiny red-eyed vireos and dark-eyed juncos went about their business with bright flickering determination; and wild turkeys moved cautiously and almost invisibly through the understory, stepping along with their ungainly yet amazingly dignified step. Darkening the skies every year were migrating flocks of geese, ducks, hawks, falcons, and, especially, hundreds of millions of passenger pigeons that annually obliterated the sun across most of eastern America.

These and a few thousand other species of plants and animals—never mind all the mushrooms, truffles, lichens, ants, mites, waterbugs, worms, flies, wasps, mosquitoes, gnats, and spiders, not to mention the unimaginably various bacterial species that festered in those rich soils—had been millions of years in the making when humans first arrived in the region. Nor was evolution done with them. Both as individual species and as ecosystems, they were constantly changing, one species giving way to another, old species dying out, new species finding niches in the biotic wall and beginning to flourish. As a collection of life forms, then, the Appalachians were still in the act of becoming when successive waves of settlement and use by human populations added a new twist to the evolutionary dance. We are still trying to understand the long-term implications of that conflation, though the evidence so far suggests that it was not an especially good thing.

Humans have been in the region for as long as 11,500 years, from Archaic times, when gathering and hunting was the only way our species had come up with to survive, to modern times, when gathering and hunting gave way to agriculture and the beginning of permanent settlements. By the time Hernan de Soto, a Spanish conquistador who, like all his ilk, lusted after gold, got himself and his bulky expedition lost in the terrifying woods of the southern Appalachians in 1540, the first peoples of the mountains had evolved into a complicated diversity of languages and cultures, from the Iroquoi and Abenaki of the north to the Cherokee and Creeks and Shawnees of the south, among many other, smaller populations. The Native American impact on the mountains was less than devastating, but it was at least measurable. They did not exactly tiptoe through the wilderness, all these people. In the north they set forest fires to enhance game and agricultural habitat and everywhere established trading networks and laced the mountains with trails connecting one community to another.

Still, this was nothing compared with what a more ambitious civilization would accomplish in the way of change. De Soto, who to his fury found no glittering treasures of gold, killed as many Indians as he could before being driven out of the mountains and on to a nasty death by disease on the banks of the Mississippi River. His successors were not long in coming. Refugees from England with colonial grants clutched in their fists were only a little less bloodthirsty, most of them, though more intent on settling the land than stripping it of treasure (that day would come). Displaying the vigor and adventuresome spirit typical of most migrating species,

Clockwise from lower left, mountain laural, Indian pink, rue anemone, Catawba rhododendron

the American colonists quickly overcame the inconvenience of coastal Indian occupation through the devices of treaties, local warfare, and—however inadvertently—disease. Soon the colonists spilled west into the coastal plain, then even farther west into the long strip of land between the Atlantic Coast and the "fall line" of the Appalachian foothills, the point at which such rivers as the James, the Potomac, the Rappahannock, the Pee Dee, and the Congaree became too turbulent for navigation and were useful mainly for the production of mill power. The region was called the piedmont, the "foot of the mountains."

Up to that point the Appalachians had served as a natural barrier to settlement in the Ohio Valley. This, the British government had decided, was only as it should be. The French and Indian War had booted the hated French out of the valley, but it was still occupied by Indians, which the government did not wish to agitate. So in 1763 the British issued a proclamation that prohibited the movement of colonials across the mountains and into the watershed of the Ohio and its tributaries. But the coastal plain and the piedmont belt were crowded now, civilized with towns and farms and roads. Land-hungry and people-burdened folk like Daniel Boone and his counterparts wanted to move on, into the land that beckoned with new hopes and opportunities on the other side of the mountains. Proclamations be damned, Indians be forewarned. Even before the American Revolution rendered British proclamations moot, Boone opened up the Wilderness Road through the Cumberland Gap from Virginia into the well-named "dark and bloody ground" of Kentucky. Down the Wilderness Road the ancestral pioneers rumbled, most of them first- or second-generation Scots-Irish or English, with their horses, cattle, sheep, pigs, dogs, seed corn, and children, spilling into the valleys and mountain coves of the plateau whose rivers flowed toward the Ohio. And so over time, settlement crept into more and more of the Appalachians' places, the people scattering and overwhelming local populations of Indians in vicious skirmishes, then scratching out a life on thousands of cornstubble farms and raising up tiny, isolated villages. Insular and clannish and deeply suspicious of anyone and anything outside the ring of family—a crotchety paranoia reinforced by all the gore that had accompanied their conquest of the mountains in the first place—the people built a life that was unique and enduring, Protestant to the bone, economically marginal, but, like most such "island" cultures, rich in language and tradition, myth and music.

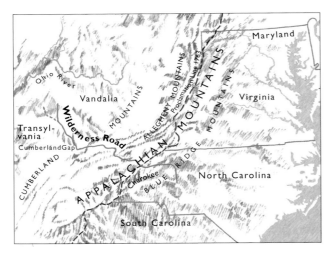

A more ambitious (if shorter-lived) kind of settlement erupted in the southern Appalachians in 1829, when a major deposit of gold was discovered on Wards Creek in northern Georgia within the boundaries of the Cherokee Nation—land that had been granted to the Cherokees by the United States in 1785 with all the usual assurances of permanence. In the light of gold's muted glitter, such assurances meant nothing. The state of Georgia rescinded the guarantees of the federal government. This was patently unconstitutional, but President

Andrew Jackson, a hardened old warrior who had done his share and more of Indian fighting, capitulated to the state's actions. By 1838 most of the Cherokee Indians had been forcibly removed from their lands, many herded along the cruel "Trail of Tears" to a new Indian Territory in Oklahoma. In the stead of Cherokee villages now were mining towns like Dahlonega, places, one observer remarked, where "drunkenness, gambling, fighting, lewdness, and every other vice" was abundant.

Indian removal 1820–1840

The gold was pretty much gone by the end of the Civil War, but by then the mountains were giving up another kind of treasure. Even in the colonial era, the great forests of northern New England had been assaulted for masts, timbers, decking, and other ship-building materials, and by the last third of the nineteenth century the northern forest, as well as the forests of the Adirondacks in New York and the Allegheny Plateau of Pennsylvania, had been systematically stripped, especially of the enormous white pines that once had defined most of these forests. Naturalist John Burroughs called it "the aboriginal tree," which, he wrote as early as 1880, "is fast disappearing from the country."

The forests of the southern Appalachians fared no better, though it took a little longer for the loggers to get there, and it was railroads, not rivers, that brought the loggers in and took the timber out—stubby, tooth-wheeled locomotives grunting noisily up and down the narrow-gauge tracks that snaked through the mountains, pulling flatcar after flatcar of big trees behind them, red spruce and fir, white pine and hemlock. It was a "war against the forest," one native complained, that left the mountains "ugly and ragged things."

Logging was not the only war in the mountains by then. In those strata laid down after the Arcadian Orogeny three or four hundred million years ago lay deposits of coal which the new age of energy needed, and by the end of the nineteenth century dirty black piles of coal-mining towns wormed their way through the hollows and narrow river valleys of the mountains from Pennsylvania into Kentucky. The coal miners and their families—most of whom derived from the original Scots-Irish settlers of the mountains—were crowded into ramshackle company housing and endured a life where electricity was rare, sanitation primitive at best, coal tipples and breakers the tallest structures in sight, the water rich in chemical spices from mine runoff, the air polluted with coal dust and stinking almost constantly from slag fires that never seemed to die.

Both coal mining and logging have survived into our own time—industrial enterprises that continue to maim the mountains where they can, especially logging. By the time World War I began, only a few stands of original old-growth forests remained, but second and third growth stands were available throughout much of the old worked-over areas within another generation. They still are. Second and third growth may be less valuable than the proud soaring groves of the past, but they nonetheless are marketable, and in forests from Moose Lake in the Longfellow Mountains of Maine to Pisgah National Forest in the Blue Ridge of North Carolina, the sound of falling trees continues to break the ancient silence of the mountains.

The View from Brasstown Bald   49

Even briefly told, the record of human activity in the Appalachians is a depressing one. The forests have been raddled, cut down by loggers and cut apart by roads; the mountains punctured and gouged and poisoned by mines; too many of the valleys urbanized and suburbanized, their plant communities disrupted, their populations of wildlife diminished alarmingly when they have not been extinguished altogether. There are no wolves or panthers or river otters now, though coyotes and maybe some wolves now appear to be filtering into Maine from Canada; red wolves have been reintroduced into the Smokies, and there is even talk of reintroducing woodland caribou in Maine. And as the chapters that follow will tell you in exquisite detail, the problems and pressures on the forests and wildlife of the mountains continue.

However, so do attempts to save what is left of both—and this too is a part of the Appalachian story. Even during the era of settlement and whole-souled exploitation there were those who loved these mountains with a finely honed passion—loved them for their own sake, for their beauty and their richness of life. Such a one was William Bartram of Virginia, a self-taught naturalist who first explored the Appalachians looking for specimens in 1775. On a peak in the Blue Ridge he looked out over a scene he said he beheld "with rapture and astonishment, a sublimely awful scene of power and magnificence, a world of mountains piled upon mountains."

Another mountain lover was Henry David Thoreau—though "love" might be too limp a word to describe the cosmic power he discovered on a stone-bald mountain-top in Maine, perhaps the exposed intrusion of some of the oldest rocks known in the land. "I looked with awe at the ground I stood on," he wrote in *The Maine Woods* more than 80 years after Bartram's wanderings. "This was that Earth of which we have heard, made out of Chaos and Old Night. Here was no man's garden, but the unhanselled globe."

John Muir, another self-taught naturalist and a refugee from a broom factory, was no less enraptured a few years after Thoreau's death in 1862—though he found gentler lessons in the land. He had decided to walk from Canada to the Gulf of Mexico to see what he could see, and on the east side of the Cumberland Gap, along the Emory River, he saw plenty. "Near this stream," he remembered, "I spent some joyous time in a grand rock-dwelling full of mosses, birds, and flowers. Most heavenly place I ever entered."

Muir—and doubtless Bartram and Thoreau—would have applauded twentieth-century efforts to rescue some "heavenly places" in the Appalachians before they were gone forever, though practicality as much as passion played a part in the effort. The importance of healthy, well-timbered watersheds in the protection of downstream civilization was well understood even by the end of the nineteenth century—not least after the experience of the 1880s, when the denuded mountains of the Allegheny Plateau sent sheets of unimpeded water down the hills, into the rivers, and ultimately into the streets of Pittsburgh and other cities in some of the worst flooding the nation had ever seen (and the most deadly; in 1889 the reservoir behind a dam above Johnstown, Pennsylvania, filled to the brim; the consequent pressure broke the dam and sent a 30-foot wall of water into town, wiping out everything in its path and killing 2,295 people). It was this understanding that had given birth to the Forest Reserve Act of 1891 and the Forest Organic

Act of 1897—both of which laid the foundation for the creation of the National Forest System and the birth of the U.S. Forest Service in 1905 with Gifford Pinchot as its head.

With the Weeks Act of 1911, which established an annual fund for the purchase of private forest land, the National Forest System now included not only western lands, but ten Appalachian forests as well—the White Mountains in Maine and New Hampshire (though mostly in New Hampshire), the Green Mountains in Vermont, the George Washington and Jefferson of Virginia, the Cherokee of Tennessee, the Pisgah and Nantahala of North Carolina, the Sumter of South Carolina, the Chattahoochee of Georgia, and the Talladega of Alabama. The forests of Maine, except for those in the state's portion of the White Mountains, remained free of federal interference and susceptible to unrestrained cutting and development. In the Adirondacks, where both a huge state park and a smaller "forest preserve" had been established in the last years of the nineteenth century, the state of New York came up with management plans that attempted to satisfy both the needs of the land and the desires of recreationists, corporate woodcutters, and resort developers.

Roaring Fork Creek, Great Smoky Mountain National Park, Tennessee

The Eastern Wilderness Act of 1975 provided a means by which at least some of the most fully recovered regions in the National Forest System in the East could be protected from roading and logging, and over the next 20 years more than thirty designated wilderness areas were established in the Appalachians, from Caribou-Speckled Mountain Wilderness in Maine–New Hampshire to the Cohutta Wilderness of Georgia. The Smokies got their own level of protection when John D. Rockefeller, Jr. combined his fortune with the millions of dimes contributed by hundreds of thousands of schoolchildren to purchase enough land to officially establish Great Smoky Mountains National Park in the 1930s, thereby preserving some of the best cove forests left in the Southern Appalachians. Shenandoah National Park in Virginia followed not long after.

Meanwhile, a lanky visionary by the name of Benton MacKaye (rhymes with "sky") had come up with something utterly new. Raised in the hamlet of Shirley Center, Massachusetts, where he would live most of his long life, and trained as a forester under Gifford Pinchot, MacKaye decided in 1921 that the Appalachians were in need of a new kind of recreational opportunity. What the mountains lacked, he told the readers of *The Journal of the American Institute of Architects*, was a path through the wilderness from Maine to Georgia, a trail on which one could "absorb the landscape and its influence as revealed in the earth," where one was encouraged "to walk, to see, and to see what you see." Eastern hiking and climbing clubs leaped at the idea and by 1925 had coalesced into the Appalachian Trail Conference. Volunteers began working with Forest Service and National Park Service officials, state park and highway agencies, and private owners, and over the next 70 years the trail was completed, with only a few minor gaps left where the hiker had to walk on the asphalt of highways or around private holdings. The Appalachian Trail was such a good idea that it gave birth to other hiking and historic trails across the land. The whole network was finally institutionalized by passage of the National Trails Act of 1968. Included in the network now is a "loop" segment recently attached to the southern end of the Appalachian Trail; the loop is called, fittingly enough, the Benton MacKaye Trail.

The Appalachian Trail still provides the best single way to discover the mountains today—particularly for those with the time and energy to walk the whole distance, something that only a few thousand people have attempted and accomplished in their lifetimes. For industrial-strength hikers, the AT is still a kind of grail. I am not an industrial-strength hiker, but I have enjoyed my walk along Moccasin Creek in Chattahoochee National Forest with Peter Kirby, a tiny expedition begun not long after he and I stood on Brasstown Bald and watched the mountains retreat like great blue waves into the distance. The land along both sides of this little stream has been proposed by conservationists as one of several additions to the National Wilderness Preservation System in the southern Appalachians, Kirby tells me. "Right now," he says, "all the designated wilderness, which comes to about 350,000 acres, together with all the roadless areas in nonwilderness lands, another 1.2 million or so, amount to only 4 percent of all land in the southern Appalachian region. Even if we get every wilderness recommendation we've made, then, we're only talking about 4 percent of the land base. Four percent. Not much."

No, it isn't much. Particularly when you take into consideration the fact that so much beauty remains uncorroded, in spite of all the generations of ecological savagery. Quite aside from what they still hold in the way of biological diversity, which is extraordinary, the Appalachians are the single greatest recreational resource left in the eastern third of the United States. More than 20 million people visit the southern Appalachians alone every year. They come here for the beauty, the life in the rivers, the trees, the sky. Where are all these people going to go to find a semblance of untrammelled nature if poisons in the air, eroded soils in the water, urban development, roading, and logging continue to degrade the land and all the life it holds? And where are their fellow nature-seekers in the northern stretches of the range going to go if every lakeside and streamside chunk of land is converted into second-home development or resort complexes; if their own spruce stands are killed off by acid deposition; if the northern forest continues to be clearcut for pulp mills?

I am thinking about all this as I plunk myself down on a flat rock on the banks of Moccasin Creek. Maybe Kirby is, too. He is leaning against a birch tree with a pensive expression on his face. The air is cool but windless here, and we both remain quiet, listening to the conversation of the creek as it leaps through a series of rocks and downed logs, swirling and foaming clean and bright and beautiful in the muted light beneath the trees—tulip poplars, hickories, and hemlocks, most of them—interspersed with clumps of rhododendron and mountain laurel. On the opposite bank of the creek, a pair of fox spar-

rows peck their way around a stretch of ground-hugging princess pine, their red rumps flashing at us. I gaze at a long curving branch of leaf-less flowering dogwood that arcs over the stream and imagine it in its spring foliage, bright creamy blossoms glowing in the darkness of the forest. I try to remember the words of a poem by the Adirondack poet, Jeanne Robert Foster. I think it may cheer Kirby up if I can recite it for him, but the words won't come and it is not until I have returned home and pulled the book out of my library that they are given back to me. Here they are:

Here in the wilderness folks will tell you
To be careful about the place you live.
For there's something in the mountains
And the hills that is stronger than people,
And you will grow like the place where you live.
The hands of the mountains reach out
With bindings that hold the heart forever.

Yes.

The Appalachians' Last Stand

How much abuse can forest trees take from airborne pollution? That is the question asked in this chapter. And where is the threshold beyond which a forest is moribund, no longer a healthy functioning ecosystem? Readers may decide for themselves, but these shocking photographs of dead trunks, dead limbs, dead leaves, dead *stands*, suggest that we are not looking at the forest-that-used-to-be in the Appalachians, that something is terribly wrong.

How did this happen? That's the next question that comes to mind, and some of the answers are given in the captions and most especially in the essay following these picture spreads. The answers have to do with acid deposition, excess nitrogen enrichment, damage from tropospheric ozone and from burning ultraviolet-B (UV-B) rays streaming through a thinning *stratospheric* ozone layer, all of which so weaken the trees that they cannot withstand the normal stresses they are subjected to as a matter of course: insects, fungi, bitter cold, and drought. Add to this a history of abysmal forest management, including generations of clearcutting and high grading, and it is scarcely a wonder that the forests of the Appalachian mountains are sick and dying.

In fact, the word *moribund* is no hyperbole, for the very soils that support the forest are sick too, depleted of their life-giving nutrients after decades of pollution-caused leaching. The same pollution transports the molecules of heavy metals into the forest, and frees a lightweight one—aluminum. Ordinarily aluminum is safely locked away in silicate compounds in the soil, but when acid deposition breaks down the compounds, the poisonous aluminum is freed to be taken up by the trees.

Where is this happening? The answer is: everywhere. Along the ridges, from Vermont to Carolina and Tennessee, the spruce and fir are dead—75 percent dead on Camel's Hump in Vermont, 80 percent dead on Mt. Mitchell in North Carolina. Downslope, the maples are in mortal decline, the ashes are yellow, the beeches are blighted, the

Standing dead Fraser fir and red spruce at Clingmans' Dome, Great Smoky Mountains National Park, Tennessee

white pines are dying of ozone, the butternut is nearly extinct, as is the red mulberry, and the hemlocks and the dogwoods are feared to be headed in the same direction. Great tracts of forests, dying.

But be careful whom you talk to about it. For there are those in government and industry who do not want this story known, who for the past 15 years have suppressed the details of the Appalachian tragedy, even dissembled about it in their testimony before the Congress of the United States. Indeed, you can find a government folder about the death of Appalachian red spruce stating that on the high ridges only 5 to 13 percent are dead. Anyone who has stood amid the devastation of pollution-killed trees on, say, Mt. Mitchell, where the gray trunks criss-cross each other like a terrible game of giant jackstraws, knows that this statistic is meant to mislead.

Do you not believe this? Well, study these pictures, read the text, and then go see for yourself. People who have a political or economic reason for suppressing the truth can manipulate statistics until they are blue in the face, but nothing can refute the commonsense evidence that any ordinary American can discover just by walking in the woods and *looking*.

Standing dead Fraser fir and red spruce, Roan Mountain, North Carolina

Where the Foggy Dew Is Fatal

For the most part, when we speak of the effects of the long-range transport of air pollutants, we call it "acid rain." But on Mt. Mitchell, socked in for up to 70 days a year, it's acid *fog* that does much of the damage.

Here the coniferous trees literally comb the acidified moisture out of the dense clouds as they sweep eastward, wetting the needles, the branches, and the trunks of the trees more thoroughly than even the hardest rain. Every part of every tree is bathed in the sour oxides of nitrogen and sulfur. In winter the effect is even more destructive. The dew freezes, holding fast against the needles and branches week after week. North Carolina State University scientists have found rime ice on Mt. Mitchell with a pH as low as 2.1, somewhere between battery acid and lemon juice.

On the exposed ridges and western slopes of Mt. Mitchell, about 80 percent of mature red spruce and Fraser fir died during the 1980s. Weakened by decades of acid deposition, they were made so vulnerable to insect infestation, drought, and hard winters that they simply succumbed. In some places, not a single large tree has survived.

Facing page, standing dead red spruce and Fraser fir, silhouetted by fog, Mt. Mitchell State Park, North Carolina

Top, a Fraser fir branch tip, and (*left*) a fir branch encased in rime ice, Mt. Mitchell State Park

A Sudden Chill in Vermont

Acid deposition operates in a very special way on coniferous trees in cold, northern climates such as Vermont's. Those wishing to minimize the effects of air pollution on the forests have claimed that ordinary "winter injury" is what has damaged red spruce and balsam fir, with the injury perhaps somewhat intensified by air pollution, but not much. University of Vermont scientists have found, however, that the story is more complicated than that.

In fact, trees weakened by years of acid deposition leaching away soil nutrients, as well as acting directly on the needles, have

Needle loss on red spruce, Mt. Ascutney, Vermont

a slower metabolism than healthy trees. Accordingly, the deep green needles whose delicate pores (called *stomata*) open up in response to warming winter sunlight—which permits the exchange of gases, oxygen for carbon dioxide—do not readily close again if the sun disappears behind a cloud on a cold, windy day.

The result is that the fluids *inside the cells* of the needles freeze solid. While conifer needles can tolerate water freezing between the cells, the freezing of the cells themselves is deadly. On the high ridges in Vermont's Green Mountains, some 75 percent of mature red spruce have died. Young trees, protected by snow cover during the winter, do not experience the same problem, which has led antienvironmentalists to claim that the impact of air pollution is no big deal. The university scientists who have been studying these effects for years know better.

"Winter injury" on red spruce needles, Vermont

A Heartache of Maples

The sugar maple, most often associated with New England, is a major canopy tree throughout the Appalachian chain. It is perhaps our most beloved eastern tree and everywhere it seems to be dying. Harvard Ayers's foreword tells the story of the dying maples on Mt. Rogers—large patches of dead trees—and his efforts to alert the Forest Service to this ecosystem breakdown. In Vermont overall sugar maple mortality has reached 35 percent. The Allegheny National Forest has been afflicted by what its supervisor has called a *full-forest decline,* with sugar maple death the most dramatic manifestation. Here, in some stands maple mortality has reached 80 percent, with the rate of regeneration down to zero.

In such places the maples starve to death, the needed soil nutrients having been leached away by decades of acid deposition, so weakening the trees that they are no longer capable of withstanding the assaults of even ordinary bad weather and diseases. As a result, the whole ecology of the forest changes. In the Alleghenies, forest scientists speculate that birch will one day become the predominant tree, given the wipeout of the sugar maple, which increased in numbers after the hemlocks, once a dominant tree, were completely removed for their tannin a century ago. And now, yet another kind of forest is to be created, less suitable than the last. And after the birch? At some point the big-tree forest will become only a memory, a heartache to recollect.

Facing page, dead sugar maple trees in an understory of brambles, Mt. Rogers, North Carolina

Above, three dead sugar maples in the Mt. Rogers National Recreation Area, Virginia

Right, sugar maple death in Allegheny State Forest, Pennsylvania

From Tailpipes to the Trees

Facing page, a healthy bigleaf magnolia in bloom, Bankhead National Forest, Alabama

In the old days, when cars were low-compression, stinky chuggers (and there were fewer of them), ozone was something you smelled after a lightning strike. Today's high-temperature, high-compression engines, while less smoky, are more dangerous—to people and to trees. The by-products are hydrocarbons and nitric oxide by the ton, which in the presence of sunlight produce ground-level or tropospheric ozone, O_3. Factory smokestacks add their bit as well.

Ozone is a chemically active form of oxygen that operates like a powerful bleach—for that is what it is. It affects the lungs of humans and causes plant foliage to die. Eventually, trees die when the cumulative effects of decades of ozone no longer allow life-giving photosynthetic processes to operate. More often, ozone-affected trees die early because in a weakened state they cannot withstand bugs, blights, or bad weather.

Laws aimed at reducing the production of tropospheric ozone are based on human-health standards, but trees are much more susceptible than people. Moreover, ozone is carried long distances and rises in altitude, killing mountain trees many miles away from a pollution source—an interstate highway, for example. The magnolia is extremely sensitive, as the photographs to the left show.

Top, mountain magnolia leaves showing tropospheric ozone damage, Ivy Knob, West Virginia

Left, close-up of ozone pathology on a mountain magnolia leaf, Ivy Knob, West Virginia

A Dangerous Moment in the Sun

Shaded leaves are less affected by ozone than those in the sun, as the photograph of the northern red oak shows. In sunlight, leaves open their stomata to exchange oxygen for carbon dioxide. But if they open during a pollution event, they absorb dam-aging ozone. Shaded leaves, whose stomata are closed, are safe, at least for the moment.

Typically, ozone damage—as shown on this page for sassafras, black gum, tulip poplar, and sourwood leaves, as well as the oak—appears as bleached patches between

the veins. While various trees—broadleafed evergreens, deciduous trees, and conifers—are susceptible to ozone damage in different degrees and in different ways, virtually all species are affected.

Top, tulip poplar, Coal River, West Virginia

Left, black gum leaves, Lilley Cornett Woods, Kentucky

Below, sassafras leaves, Coal River, West Virginia

Bottom, sourwood leaves, Ivy Knob, West Virginia

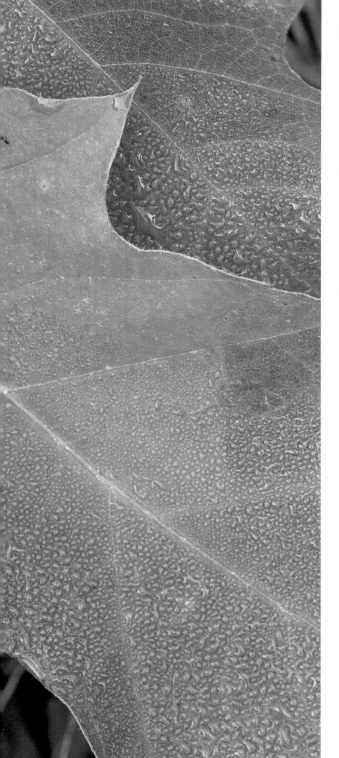

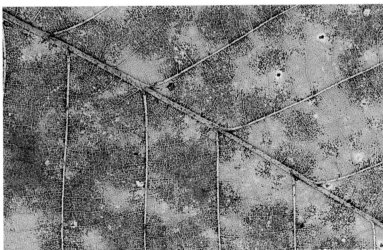

Top, shagbark hickory on the Wills' property, Rock Creek Hollow, West Virginia

Above, close-up of shagbark hickory leaf and *(right)* a branch from the same tree showing possible UV-B damage

UV-B and the Other Ozone

Composed of the same molecule as the tropospheric ozone described on the previous pages, *stratospheric* ozone forms a "shield" to protect the earth from the bombardment of damaging ultraviolet rays in the "B" range—a shorter wavelength than the ultraviolet rays that give us suntans and make the sky blue.

Without the stratospheric ozone shield, life on earth would be perilous for humans, if not impossible, because UV-B causes blindness and cancer. Discovered to be thinning in the southern hemisphere in the late 1970s, the ozone shield has also been affected in the northern hemisphere, including the United States, by rising chlorofluorocarbons, mainly the Freon of air conditioners and aerosol cans, which break down the O_3 molecule.

The pictures on this page show the impacts of a 1995 UV-B bombardment event in West Virginia on both deciduous and coniferous trees. The blotchy and wrinkled UV-B burns on the hickory leaf are different from cell damage produced by tropospheric ozone, although chlorophyll bleaching may also be present on the leaf. Even more telling and definite is the effect of UV-B on white pine needles, here shown uncharacteristically bent and lying flat along the branch. This is from UV-B burn damage to the tender base needles as they emerge, causing a scarring that hardens the exposed side, which in turn produces an abnormal deflection as the needle grows to maturity.

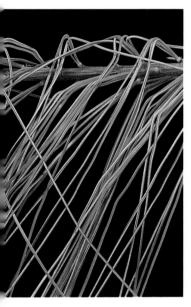

White pine (*right*) on the Aliff property in Rock Creek, West Virginia, with UV-B-affected branch and needles (*above*)

Autumn in July

Branch dieback on northern red oak, Blue Ridge Parkway, Virginia

Sometimes in the polluted woods of the Appalachians, it seems as if the fall comes earlier and earlier every year. Branch dieback, premature leaf-drop, and thinning crowns can be found afflicting a large number of different species on sites at every elevation all along the Appalachians, from Vermont to Virginia and beyond.

The thinning of leaves and crowns not only affects the health of the trees themselves but eventually changes the very composition of the woods. Increases in light reaching the forest floor encourage the heavy growth of ferns, raspberries, and other plants that can so thoroughly shroud the soil beneath them that many trees do

not regenerate—sometimes because the seeds do not reach the ground, sometimes because the acid-base balance of the soil is changed, sometimes because seedlings of the dominant trees cannot tolerate the changed light conditions.

Below, premature leaf-drop on quaking aspens near Woodstock, Vermont

Bottom, thinning crown of a sugar maple, Hueston Woods, Ohio

Snaps and Topples
in the Falling Forest

A complex of stresses, with air pollution
playing a major role, allows accelerated
fungal invasion of weakened forest trees.
"Conks" of various kinds on the trunks of
living trees are a mature form of fungus.
The *Armillaria* fungus shown at left is deadly
only after other stresses take their toll.

Nowhere is the impact of fungus on
pollution-stressed trees more pronounced
than in the mixed mesophytic forest of
West Virginia and Kentucky, where large
areas are littered with trees that have
snapped off halfway up the trunk, or simply
turned over, toppled "like an old tooth," as
landowner Joe Aliff has put it, their roots
rotted away. Science writer John Flynn, to
whom this book is dedicated, wrote about
this phenomenon in woodlands of the Coal
River Valley of West Virginia, calling it
"the falling forest."

Top, Armillaria fungus
under bark of tree,
Allegheny National
Forest, Pennsylvania

Fungus conk on a live
sugar maple, Hueston
Woods, Ohio

Below, a tipped-over tulip
poplar, with rotted roots,
on Aliff's property, Rock
Creek, West Virginia

A Cascade of Consequences

Although air pollution is rarely the primary cause of the death of forest trees in the Appalachians, its weakening effect makes various species vulnerable to all manner of creatures and environmental conditions that can cause their demise. All too often, U.S. foresters, reflecting the political and economic interests of those who sign their paychecks, wish to minimize the importance of air pollution's impacts on the eastern forests, asserting that the *proximate* cause of tree death and forest decline is the *only* cause. According to this view, the fatal webworm and adelgid damage, the beech scale, the gypsy moth defoliation shown on these pages is the whole story, having nothing to do with air pollution.

The idea that the death of so many different species of trees along the Appalachian chain is simply happenstance—a coincidental aggregation of isolated, anomalous events—seriously challenges ordinary logic. Today even the most cautious forest scientists now confirm that the death and decline of Appalachian trees and forests is from a cascade of consequences whose point of origin, at least in part, is the debilitating effect, year after year, of air pollution from distant cities, factories, and highways.

Facing page, webworms and locust leaf borers, Shenandoah National Park, Virginia

Above, dead red spruce and Fraser fir, Great Smoky Mountains National Park, Tennessee

Left, beech scale in an old-growth woods at Hearts Content, Allegheny National Forest, Pennsylvania

Below, gypsy moth caterpillar defoliation, Shenandoah National Park, Virginia

A dead eastern hemlock on White Canyon Trail, Shenandoah National Park, Virginia

The Bug that Feeds on Pollution

Throughout most of the Appalachians, remnant stands of hemlocks, as well as individual trees such as the formerly magnificent specimen shown here, are dying at an increasing rate from an infestation of the hemlock woolly adelgid. The adelgid is a pinhead-sized creature that during the winter, when the hemlock is stressed from cold, sucks the tree's sap and simultaneously injects a toxic saliva into the tissue. A heavily infested tree will die within 1–4 years. The telltale evidences of infestation are the fuzzy white egg sacs deposited by the female on the undersides of newly grown outer branches.

An import from Asia, the adelgid has been around for nearly a half-century in eastern forests without causing undue destruction until recently. Today hemlock death is so widespread that some fear the species will become locally extinct in the wild. The reason for the sudden virulence may well be that the insect thrives on nitrogen, an excess of which results from deposition of pollutants. Experiments have shown that when nitrogen is applied to adelgid-infested hemlocks, the population densities of the pest increase fivefold compared with infested trees not subject to abnormal amounts of nitrogen.

Ovisacs with eggs of hemlock woolly adelgid

A Dimming Light

Suddenly, beginning in the late 1970s, the dogwoods began dying. First in Connecticut, then southward down the mountains in a plague that moved faster than any other. Though the dogwood has no economic value (except to nurserymen, at least before the plague), people have always admired the way the little tree lights up the woods in early spring with its creamy-white bracts—the leaflike coverings that open to reveal the actual blossom, which is insignificant. In places where the plague has run its course, some 80 percent of the dogwoods have succumbed. In especially hard-hit areas, such as parts of Maryland's Catoctin Mountains, 100 percent of the dogwoods have died.

The cause is *anthracnose*, a fungus infection that hits many trees, including the dogwood. Ordinarily, while anthracnose discolors some of the leaves, it usually does no permanent harm. Indeed, most dogwoods are affected by "spot" anthracnose every year. But now a different kind of anthracnose is loose—a killer. After a long study, mycologists have described it as an entirely new species—unknown in North America, Europe, or Asia. Appropriately named *Discula destructiva*, the fungus is especially virulent in dogwood trees weakened by air pollution.

Springtime brings a spray of dogwood blossom in Great Smoky Mountains National Park, Tennessee

Anthracnose on a dogwood branch at the University of Tennessee Arboretum, Oak Ridge

The View that Doesn't Go on Forever

The view on a clear day of Dickey Ridge, from an overlook in the northern section of Shenandoah National Park, Virginia. Visibility is between 50 and 75 miles

Why the trees are dying and the forests declining in the Appalachians becomes perfectly obvious to any visitor taking in the view from a scenic turnout along nearly any mountain ridge, as this pair of photographs shows.

Before being obscured by pollutants from distant sources, visibility from peaks in the central and southern Appalachians was nearly a hundred miles on the average. Today it averages about 25 miles, with visibility on the very worst days, which

occur during the summer months, only a tenth of that.

Sulfate-based aerosol particles are the main culprit, and though this constituent of air pollution is decreasing in most areas of the country thanks to 1990 amendments to the Clean Air Act, in the southern Appalachians sulfate is still slightly on the increase. Nitrogen, by contrast, which in the presence of sunlight creates Los Angeles-type smog, is not being controlled seriously and has increased rapidly. Even with anticipated sulfate reductions from stricter air pollution legislation, visibility is expected to increase only by about 4 miles in the summertime. It would seem that the views that once went on forever in the Appalachians will remain shrouded.

Same view when affected by air pollution. Visibility is reduced to between 3 and 10 miles

Appalachian Sunset

The only thing that can mar a beautiful sunset over the Appalachians is its color—a vivid mauve is a sign that deadly pollution is probably hanging over this venerable range of mountains, affecting not only the ridges as it sweeps across the summits on prevailing winds, but the midelevation valleys, coves, and hollows as well.

Scarcely any part of these mountains is unaffected by the emissions of factories, power plants, vehicles, city air conditioners—emissions that result in acid deposition in the form of rain, fog, rime ice, and snow; as well as tropospheric ozone, excess nitrogen, even UV-B bombardment. A chemical soup, together with altered weather patterns from global warming, not only weakens the trees, but also steals the future vitality of the forest by depleting its soils of vital nutrients and changing its original biological makeup. For an authoritative account of the complex mechanisms at work, the reader should attend closely the following essay by one of our most distinguished forest ecologists, Orie Loucks.

Yes, the Appalachian sunsets are beautiful. However, they are terrifying too, for they suggest a tragedy in the making unless we can resolutely and quickly reduce the impacts of pollution on the forest, from Camel's Hump in Vermont, clear to Gregory Bald in Tennessee.

The end of the day at Gregory Bald, Great Smoky Mountains National Park, Tennessee

In Changing Forests, A Search for Answers

by Orie Loucks

In May 1991, I remember climbing through white basswood, yellow buckeye, tulip poplars, hickory, and black gum in a high cove on the north-facing slope of Rock Creek Hollow. This was my first trip to southern West Virginia and I was to make many more. But in just the past 24 hours I had seen 70 species of trees and tall shrubs—an astonishing variety compared with most eastern woodlands. Above us, on the upper side-crest of a ridge, there was old-growth beech, red oak, and sugar maple. Above that on the narrow ridge-top were 20- to 30-inch black, white, and chestnut oaks. The ridge-top trees were not tall, but they provided a remarkable counterpoint to trees of different species just 200 feet downslope, free of side branches, and over 100 feet tall.

I was visiting these species-rich mountain forests on the recommendation of a friend, John Flynn, with whom I had worked when he wrote on the effects of acid deposition in the Midwest. He had returned to his boyhood home in West Virginia and was surprised by the numbers of dead and dying trees throughout the hollows. He had talked with other landowners in the area, older men such as Joe Aliff, the owner of the site we were visiting. He and others I visited later had decades of familiarity with the forest. They all told us the same thing: branch dieback and mortality in a few species had begun some 25 years earlier and accelerated in number of species affected and overall decimation up to the present time. Flynn knew that research on air pollution effects in forests, my own work included, suggested that damage from acid deposition would be most likely on the low-nutrient sandstone ridges. Effects from long-term exposures to ground-level ozone, another serious pollutant, also could be more serious on the exposed, high-elevation ridges than in the hollows. But the local observers were seeing more mortality and decline in the rich coves and upper slopes than on the ridges, and they were asking why. They had asked me to come and see their forest, and I had been glad to try to help if I could.

I will come back to what we found shortly, but first let me provide background on why I was interested in these forests scientifically, beginning many years ago in Canada. Indeed this old-growth hardwood forest in West Virginia reminded me of my own early years, growing up in the hemlock-hardwood forests of central Ontario near the southernmost reaches of the Canadian shield. My great-grandfather, his two brothers and a brother-in-law, each took out 100-acre land grants in 1867, building log homes and barns. In fact, one barn still remains in limited use. Each retained a few stands of old-growth

Red spruce, Mt. Mitchell State Park, North Carolina

maple, beech, hemlock, and yellow birch—part sugarbush, part cash crop to be used in emergencies, but also a living thing of beauty in an otherwise bleak and rocky landscape. For our annual fuelwood needs, rather than cut living trees from his 100 acres of remnant old growth, my father, who had acquired all the older relatives' lands, always had places in the second-growth forest where trees could be removed.

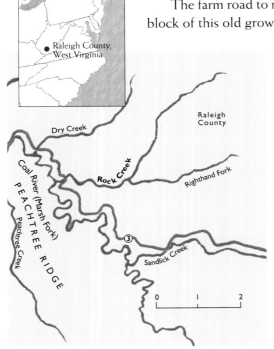

The farm road to my one-room school wound through the largest block of this old growth, and I walked it twice a day in the late 1930s to early 1940s, seeing it in all seasons. In winter the snow layer served so well as a protective, warming blanket that when my father needed fresh soil to bank around the maple-sugaring pans in March, there was no frost. In spring, as the tips of tree roots and below-ground buds of spring herbs were swollen and primed for rapid growth, the choreography of tree flowering and fruiting began—from the early red maples, willows, and aspen to the later crops of ironwood and oak, a repeating element of my youthful lessons from the woods. Each fall, the art class at school focused in some new way on the colored foliage. One year we made collages of carefully pressed and dried leaves, another we sketched in color pencil, and still another painted the landscape in watercolors. I learned every detail of healthy fall foliage and the difference from midsummer, drought-induced coloring and leaf-fall. Working with my father after school and most weekends to cut fuelwood, and occasionally prime logs for sale, I learned to read the surface indicators of tree-trunk condition and of log quality like a book, the way my father did. Routinely, I counted the rings of the largest trees we cut with an old two-man crosscut saw. Some of the sugar maples were nearly 400 years old.

It was no surprise then, that at the University of Toronto in 1949, I began study for what turned out to be two degrees in the science of forestry. It was probably also no surprise that I took summer jobs in the broadleaf forests of the southern Canadian Shield, in timber surveys one year of all the age classes in the region, as a naturalist in Algonquin Park another year, and in research at the nearby University of Toronto Forest in still another. These brought further enrichment in my understanding of tree species and the characteristics of old-growth forests. Later I was to learn about young forests and how they relate developmentally to old growth.

In the 1960s, when I was teaching at the University of Wisconsin, my graduate students sampled a series of age classes on rich soils of the former Menominee Indian Reservation. Here, 30-year-old aspen, grown up following a fire, sheltered white pine saplings and occasional ash and oak in a new stand beneath the aspen canopy; 130-year pine and oak forests had traces of aspen remaining, and saplings of hemlock underneath; 300-year pine forests, 36 inches in diameter and 140 feet tall, had hemlocks 80 feet high in the understory, with sugar maples and yellow birch to 60 feet. One site, supporting hemlocks aged to 370 years, yielded a single pine stump and log that we were able to date to a fire 475 years earlier. Indeed, northern Wisconsin's natural landscape could be seen as a mosaic of age classes, each with different species composition, determined by the pattern of fires and windstorms, which returned at intervals of 70 to 700 years. In those days I wrote and spoke often about the evolution of each tree species capitalizing on the opportunities for regeneration afforded by the repetition over millions of years of this temporal disturbance pattern. We were finding that forests, like elephants, have a remarkable record of their own history, if we are wise enough to read it. Clearly, the pattern of dependence on disturbance that we had uncovered was ancient. It had ended, for the most part, with the arrival of white settlement.

For hemlock forest, the pattern over time by which seedlings, saplings, and thus trees become established also was of critical interest. We asked whether, after 300 years or more, the forest might still have an even-aged character, derived from its disturbance origin, or might have developed an all-aged structure, based on the ability of the seedlings to survive and develop under the shade of a mature stand. The results showed that the forest had seedlings from nearly every one of the 30 or more decades of its development. We also found that the number of stems in each age class followed a negative-exponential decline from the youngest to the oldest classes, confirming that stems in every age class have the constant probability of death over their lifetime that nearly all plant species have.

Other scientists, however, were finding that in less wind- and fire-prone landscapes, especially the high-rainfall areas of the Appalachians and the Northeast, the processes of forest renewal were more subtle. Work by Herbert Bormann of Yale University, Gene Likens of the Cary Arboretum, and James Runkle of Wright State University in Ohio had shown that "small gap" dynamics, where one or a few trees may die or be blown down, leads to replacement by a small patch of seedlings representing pioneer species, as seen in Wisconsin, as well as the shade-tolerant mature forest species. The forest as a whole could be seen as a fine-grained mosaic, stable in terms of its structure (i.e., the distribution of its biomass from crown to roots), its species composition, and the probabilities of sapling and tree mortality. The remarkable process of renewal was about the same as in Wisconsin in principle, but the disturbances and the renewal of trees had to be searched for carefully. In many areas, of course, dynamics at both local and large scales could be found within an immediate landscape, illustrated by fires of moderate scale and frequency, and somewhat even-aged forests on upper slopes and ridges, while all-aged gap dynamics operated on nearby lower slopes and sheltered coves.

Accordingly, in my visits to West Virginia forests beginning in the early 1990s, I was looking for the pattern of age classes characteristic of each site and species, for the natural disturbance agents associated with some forms of forest renewal, and for the indicators of a healthy forest as I had learned them years earlier in Canada. I was looking for flowering and fruiting vigor, for the width of annual growth rings, for bole and bark characteristics, the distribution and density of summer foliage, the expression of fall colors, and the distribution of age classes for each species. But what I found in West Virginia surprised me, and not simply because the region was somewhat new to me. There were anomalies of crown density and branch dieback patterns that I had come to see during the 1980s in Indiana and Ohio, and in Ontario where all the larger trees in my great-grandfather's sugarbush had died in the '80s. I was aware of, and had studied, the "new forest death" in spruce, beech, and oak forests of Europe, and the many changes in soil chemistry, from acid deposition, that accounted for the European forest decline. Forest ecologists in the United States were asking themselves, could acid deposition also change the soils of the highly diverse hardwood forests here, enough to cause decline and mortality patterns comparable to those seen in Europe?

An opportunity to understand scientifically the possible relationship of pollution to changes in broadleaf forests along the Ohio Valley had presented itself in the late 1980s when several colleagues and I were awarded a multiyear grant by the Forest Response Program of the National Acid Precipitation Assessment Program (NAPAP). The first step in testing hypotheses about the effects of acid deposition on forest trees required determining both current and historical deposition amounts, and the concentrations of related pollutants such as ground-level ozone. For those concerned with such matters, our study design utilized a gradient in the deposition of sulfate ions from a relatively low-dose site in southern Illinois (historically) to higher-dose sites in southern Indiana and Ohio. We found fairly even steps in acid ion inputs between each of the three states for cumulative deposition of nitrate and sulfate during the past eight decades, with the aggregate difference being some 2.5 equivalents per square meter of soil surface. Fortunately, there were no differences in the growing-season ozone concentrations along the gradient.

In each state along the west-to-east gradient, then, we sampled the soils on very similar sandstone-derived parent material, keeping all the sites south of the maximum glacial advance. We found differences in the soils along the gradient consistent with an acid "titration" effect on soil bases due to acidic deposition: the eastern sites (Indiana and Ohio), with the longest period of high deposition and greatest cumulative dose, had significantly lower pH in the surface mineral (A1) horizon (pH 4.0 compared with 4.7 at the lower dose Illinois site); and the B horizon of the highest dose site (Edge-of-Appalachia in Ohio) also showed significantly lower total bases and much lower base saturation than the Illinois reference site. The lower level of essential bases, such as calcium, on the high-dose sites was proportional to the gradient in 80-year cumulative deposition of nitrogen and sulfate ions. But, in addition, high levels of exchangeable aluminum were now present in the soils at those high-dose sites. The resulting ratio of calcium to aluminum was significantly lower at the eastern sites, an indicator of potential toxicity to tree roots and other organisms.

As for biological responses to the changes in soil chemistry, our studies of soil animals, specifically short-lived species closely linked to their surrounding soil chemistry, showed greatly reduced abundances in the high-dose sites (Indiana and Ohio) compared with southern Illinois. Physiologically based modeling showed that the decline in number of earthworms, from 30 per square meter to 1 per square me-

ter, from Illinois to Ohio, could be explained entirely by the change in soil pH. As for the differences in total mass and overall respiration of the soil organisms, we found the highest-dose site had only 30 percent of the animal life in that of a reference site in Illinois. Indeed, there had been local extinction of half of the soil animal species. All of these changes were consistent with scientific results from aquatic ecosystems for the same level of pH change.

Did the lower soil pH resulting from the transport and deposition of pollutants on the west-to-east prevailing winds, along with the loss of soil animals, make any difference to the trees? To answer this, we looked at changes during the past 60 years in the basal area increment (BAI) of trees, using 30 duplicate tree-ring cores for each of three tree species. The change in the BAI trend (which in healthy forests is upward—or at least level—between 1934–1960 and 1960–1987) showed that up to 33 percent of the surviving black oak and 24 percent of the white oak exhibited post-1960 growth decline at the sites where the ratio of calcium to aluminum was low. No white oak and only 5 percent of the black oak showed decline at sites with moderate calcium to aluminum ratios. Reconstructed dating of all the dead trees observed showed that tree mortality rates were significantly higher during the 1978–87 decade in comparison with 1968–77, despite little difference in weather. Mortality had been greater for the black oak-red oak group of species than for the white oak group. However, mortality was rather similar from Illinois to Ohio, undoubtedly because, as a key criterion in choosing the sample plots, we avoided stands in which mortality was noticeably present.

Given these findings, we concluded that the pattern of differences observed in the sandstone-derived soils of this Ohio Corridor region were consistent with hypotheses linking acidic deposition to soil changes and related forest health. The long-term, high levels of sulfur inputs, together with the more recent high levels of nitrogen deposition, apparently had induced soil changes predisposing the forest to increased incidence of a decline in individual tree growth, and even increased mortality during the last decade.

Unfortunately, the study results from upper-slope soils on sandstone along the Midwestern gradient did not really explain the high mortality I was seeing in the high cove hardwoods of West Virginia in 1991. These were high-nutrient soils, dark in color, and rich in organic matter. The ridge-top trees showed some branch decline and mortality, as they did in Indiana and Ohio, but not as much as in the cove forests below. I was seeing evidence of profound changes in the West Virginia forests, but that evidence was at odds with the whole acid rain paradigm we had studied along the Ohio Valley: If acid deposition was ever to induce change, it would be seen for the most part on the low-base sandstone-derived soils of the ridge tops. While that hypothesis seemed to hold in the Ohio Valley study, where we had sampled only upper slopes and ridges, it obviously was insufficient for what was occurring in West Virginia. Clearly, other mechanisms of change must be operating. Soils of the type we saw in the coves had not been investigated by anyone during the Forest Response Program, because our limited understanding at the time suggested that these forests would be healthy.

I reviewed in my mind the hypotheses that included mechanisms for forest decline on high-nutrient soils. The most obvious was the high ground-level ozone, a region-wide pollutant known to produce serious negative effects on crops, such as soybeans and vegetables, as well as on human health. Seedlings of several tree species were known to be sensitive to ozone, but most of the species in the mountains had not been tested. Many studies, I knew, had shown already that ozone affects trees by oxidizing photosynthetic products (carbohydrate) in the foliage, reducing the stored carbon otherwise available for a grain crop, or in trees, for storage in tree trunks and for the growth of roots. Several studies had linked the reduction in root carbohydrates (due to ozone) to an increased sensitivity of affected trees to moderate drought events. Another projected result was an increased sensitivity to attack by defoliating insects and stem diseases during or following such a drought. There was a reasonable hypothesis that high levels of ground-level ozone could induce the changes in the high cove forests I was seeing, but little was known yet about the sensitivity of species such as white basswood, yellow buckeye, and the hickories. I still could hardly imagine what the experimental approaches would be for answering questions about reduced carbon translocation from canopy to roots in mature broadleafed trees, or the increased risk from reduced root systems during drought events, for individuals of these and other species.

Other evidence came to mind, however, for considering yet another hypothesis to account for damage in rich cove forests. Nitrogen (N) enrichment was universal in the mountains, from the high rainfall and greatly increased levels of N in modern rain. Industry reviewers of the NAPAP final reports had insisted on including reports of the growth-enhancing benefits of N in acid-altered rainfall. Despite a small reduction sought for N emissions during the 1990s, no long-term cap on nitrogen had been set in the Clean Air Act Amendments passed by Congress in 1990. But two new areas of concern about nitrogen enrichment were opening up: First, studies in Europe were focused on setting a "critical load" or target limit for N deposition, above which there was a high risk of negative effects and the possibility of long-term forest collapse. Second, studies of high-carbon "secondary metabolites," compounds formed in healthy leaves grown where there is moderate competition for N, were showing these compounds to be critical for defense against insect and disease attack. The N addition in rainfall, while initially increasing aboveground "growth" in some species, was being seen as sufficient to change the carbon-to-nitrogen ratio of foliage, reducing the formation of high-carbon secondary metabolites, and reducing defenses against insects and disease. These mechanisms appeared to explain the long-term collapse of forests attributed by several authors to N enrichment.

By the late summer of 1992, I had found forest decline in many more areas of the Appalachian Mountains. A paper by the U.S. Forest Service (USFS) had described unusual levels of mortality in an important nature preserve, Dick's Cove, Tennessee. This was a remnant of old growth in what the pioneering botanist E. Lucy Braun had named the mixed mesophytic forest, the highly diverse forest of the Cumberland Mountains of Tennessee and Kentucky, and the Allegheny Plateau of West Virginia, Ohio, and Pennsylvania. I wanted very much to see more of the sites that Braun had studied in the 1930s. I needed to explore fully the evidence for more frequent droughts and fires in what she called the western mesophytic oak and hickory region to the west of the mountains, and the drought- and fire-adapted oak-chestnut region she had identified for the ridge-and-valley and Blue Ridge mountains to the east.

One of these places was the 500-acre old-growth Lilley Cornett Preserve in the Cumberland Mountains of southeastern Kentucky. The site had been purchased by Mr. Cornett soon after World War I to prevent its being logged. I could see some of my own grandfather's vision in his foresight. Fifty years later the forest had become a Kentucky State Natural Area. As in West Virginia, the rich slopes, with basswood, tulip poplar, beech, oak, and hickory showed the greatest evidence of premature blow-downs, snap-offs and standing dead trees. The changes were the more remarkable here because of the evidence over such a large area, and with the remaining trees being so straight and tall, the opening up now was making the forest susceptible to further insect attack and blowdown. The Lilley Cornett forest is remarkable also because the stand and understory here is characterized by four species of magnolia, those primitive but beautiful tree-layer associates from the age of dinosaurs. I was struck by the contradiction between antiquity, represented by the number of primitive angiosperm (flowering) trees in this forest, and the modern threat to it from anthropogenic pollutants. These species, or their immediate ancestors, had survived the great meteoric implosion, dust cover, and climate change at the end of the Cretaceous Era 60 million years ago, but I wondered if they would survive the effects of *Homo sapiens* in the twenty-first century A.D.

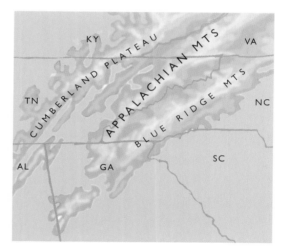

Clearly, we needed to know the full geographic scope of the changes evident in the mountains of West Virginia, southern Ohio, Kentucky, and Tennessee. The U.S. Forest Service and each state maintain a system of forest inventory plots, with scheduled re-measurements to detect changes in growth or mortality. The trouble is, the interval between remeasurement of these plots is 10 to 18 years. The most recent measurements in some states were 10 years old, and the midpoint between the last two remeasurements (the applicable date for a mortality determination) would be some years prior to that. We needed current measurements to tell us what was happening year by year in the 1990s. With the grassroots interest of local forest owners and others, however, we seemed to have the possibility of using "citizen science" volunteers to establish a large number of permanent plots that local people could measure and remeasure, thereby getting current data on the condition of the forest. With funding from the Moriah Foundation and others to support training, data quality assurance, and compilation, 224 plots in seven mountain states from Alabama to Pennsylvania were established during the years 1994–96 and monitored by our citizen-scientists.

What did we learn from these current, region-wide data? First, we found that, on the average, the mortality rate in the mountains is 1.6 percent of the cross-sectional basal area of trees each year. This is three times the natural rate of mortality in old-growth forests, 0.5 percent per year, that I had calculated several years ago, and three times the rate of mortality that my colleague Bruce McCune had reported for long-term remeasurements prior to the 1980s.

Does a threefold change in mortality matter? In very simple terms one can think of a 1.6 percent annual rate as being 16 percent of the forest lost each decade, or 160 percent in 100 years (although there are nonlinearities to be considered over this long time span). Obviously, mortality at more than 100 percent per century leaves a forest with the oldest trees mostly less than 100 years old. In contrast, forests historically appear to have had a mortality rate of 5 percent per decade, or roughly 50 percent per century, leaving a substantial portion of the trees of many species to age for a second and third century, as we know was the case at the time of settlement. For the internal gap processes and renewal in these forests, the frequency or extent of openings now would be increased by threefold, greatly increasing light in the understory, leading to long-term dominance by shrubs and vines, and reducing the survival rates for ground-layer seedlings and herbs. Ecologists call this the "cascading" effect.

Other interesting patterns were evident in the 1994–96 citizen-science measurements. First, we compared the mortality rates from the dry ridges with results for fresh and moist (cove) sites. As expected from casual observation, the dry sites showed the lowest mortality rate (but double historic rates, comparable to our Ohio Corridor results), while fresh and moist sites showed mortality of 2.0 percent per year. But also, as expected, we found a gradient in mortality rate from the uplands of northern Alabama (with lower pollution levels than farther north) to the high-dose mountains of West Virginia and Pennsylvania. Also evident was a gradient from the generally low mortality rates in the lower elevation (~400 m) forests of central Kentucky to high mortality rates in the roughly 800-m broadleaf forests of West Virginia. This gradient was consistent with the even more serious damage to spruce forests documented by NAPAP for the highest elevations of New England and North Carolina.

Still, some colleagues were concerned whether a tree-death rate of 0.5 percent per year was truly the natural rate for a broad range of species and age classes, and whether a short-period excursion into high rates of mortality might not be a natural phenomenon due to the internal dynamics of second-growth forests so widespread in the eastern United States. They argued that it was essential to understand the role of drought events, introduced diseases, and defoliating insects, such as the gypsy moth, before we could conclude that the changes being seen might be attributed to air pollutant loads.

An outcome of these conversations was that first John Flynn, and later Bill Grant, a scientist at NASA–Langley in Virginia, obtained several dozen of the state and federal reports on the USFS's Forest Inventory and Analysis plot remeasurements. These plots were first established on a consistent large-scale basis in the post-World War II years and remeasured three or more times since then. The reports included data on the tree mortality between each remeasurement. We wanted to test the null hypothesis that no trend in mortality rate was present, and believed this could be tested over the period 1950 to 1995 using the USFS plot data. We found there were 10 eastern states with published records for three or more remeasurement intervals. The mortality rate for oak and hickory species in these states (based on several thousand plots) ranged from 0.2 to 0.8 percent per year on a volume basis up to the mid-1960s. The average rate was 0.5 percent per year at that time. By the early 1990s, hickory mortality averaged 1.33 percent per year, while white oak was 1.05 percent per year.

Obviously, the annual mortality in these forests had changed since the 1960s, but understanding whether the change was natural or from some human cause required a deeper assessment. Drought events were a possible factor, but we found no trend toward more severe droughts over these 40 years in the study area. Severe wind events and ice storms can also produce local mortality, but these remained essentially random over time. The natural aging of the forest could be argued as an explanation, because most of these eastern forests are relatively young (having been burned, logged heavily, or otherwise disturbed one or more times during the past 120 years), and now average only 50 to 90 years old. Older growth is present only in scattered pockets. Historically, the oaks and hickories here were not thought to be physiologically mature until 200 to 300 years old, and such age classes still characterize the remnant old-growth sites. The recent 30-year aging interval (1960 to 1990), leading to the present 50- to 90-year forest, is not a plausible basis for a sudden increase in death rate due to aging.

Internal stand dynamics, on the other hand, which my students in Wisconsin had studied in detail, could lead to pulses of high mortality within second-growth forests through aging, competition, and thinning. Competition between trees during early stand development can lead to the death of large numbers of pole-sized trees. However, the cross-sectional basal area or volume of these suppressed stems is not large and would not be a major part of the volume-based USFS plot inventory result shown in the following graphs. Understory trees

We looked first at possible correlations between pollutant loads in the late 1980s, and the reported mortality of red oak (and black oak) and white oak species in 12 northeastern and mid-Atlantic states.

down to 13 cm in diameter are included in the plot inventory data, and would naturally show short periods of high mortality, and stems in the 25- to 50-cm diameter range occasionally can be subject to shading and death from competition. However, upper canopy trees, particularly those in all-aged stands, experience little suppression and have the low, relatively constant probability of death that I had found in Wisconsin. But the new data from the citizen-science surveys showed that from West Virginia to Alabama, 72 percent of the oak and hickory trees that died between 1985 and 1995, on a cross-sectional basal-area basis, were free-growing upper canopy trees (assuming that half the trees of 25-50 cm in diameter, and all those of 50 cm and up are dominants or codominants). This could not be the result of internal stand dynamics. Fluctuation in the mortality rate due to stand dynamics could be a cause of the variation about the mean in each decade shown on the graph, but could in no way be the explanation for the more than doubling of the mean over 40 years in such a large geographic area.

Other causes of oak mortality during this century have been proposed by many authors, most finding that the Appalachian Mountain region seems always to have had scattered areas of decline and mortality due to insect and disease attacks, with no evident time trend. Several occurrences of "oak decline" were reported over portions of a few

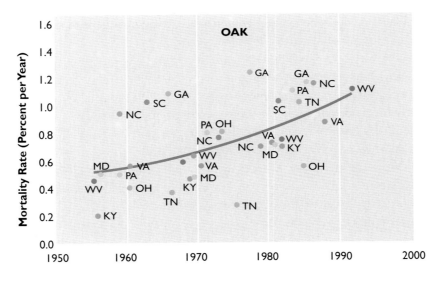

Mortality rates for two species obtained from multiple measurements of forest inventory plots from 1950 to 1995. Each point represents the average annual mortality rate in each state for the period between resurveys, and is placed at the midpoint of the interval. The line represents the average mortality of the species in the ten and nine states respectively.

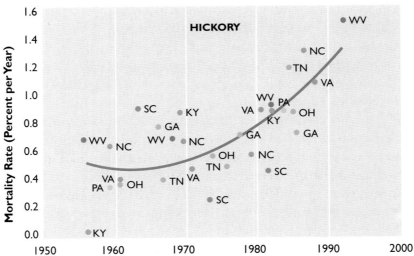

states in earlier decades, but never over a 10-state area. More recently, an introduced defoliator, the gypsy moth, has attacked oak, hickory, and other species in the Northeast. It spread during the USFS plot resurveys through northern portions of the region represented on the graph, but not significantly into southern West Virginia, Kentucky, or Tennessee. Could it have caused the trend toward increased mortality? When data from states that have not been affected by gypsy moth are removed from the diagram and considered separately, the trend over time for hickory and oak mortality is not different in any way from the trend in states defoliated by gypsy moths. If defoliation were to be the explanation for mortality in a few states, then what is the explanation in the unaffected states? The principle of parsimony states that in such cases an underlying cause that may have affected both groups of states must be sought.

The search for an underlying cause led us to ask whether the pattern of increasing deposition of air pollutants since the 1950s, including ground-level ozone and acid ion deposition, explained the pattern and trend in mortality. We looked first at possible correlations between pollutant loads in the late 1980s, and the reported mortality of red oak (and black oak) and white oak species in 12 northeastern and mid-Atlantic states. Red oak mortality proved to correlate closely with ozone dose, but not with deposition of the acid ions. White oak mortality correlated marginally with acid ion deposition, but not with ozone. This finding of a difference in sensitivity between red and white oaks to acid ion inputs and ground-level ozone dose is precisely what the majority of previous growth-chamber studies had shown.

We also found that, for all hickory species growing in 16 midwestern and mountain states, ground-level ozone was the only pollutant strongly correlated with annual mortality rate. A test for all oak species (including data from the southeastern states where oak species were left undifferentiated in the inventory plot reports) showed ground-level ozone to be the factor of overwhelming significance for explaining the observed mortality. Our analysis also evaluated USFS plot inventory data used in an assessment of "oak decline" in 10 southern states. A very high correlation was obtained, again with ozone dose, although a multiple correlation using ozone and the two acid ions showed that the latter are capable of providing an additional explanation of the mortality data. All of these results are supported by years of growth-chamber and field experiments showing that ozone damage and soil chemistry changes can alter the metabolism of whole trees. When these results are considered with the correlative evidence above, there is little doubt that air pollutants, in different combinations for different species and areas, are the critical factors explaining changes in the Appalachian forests.

But we were finding, too, that these high-diversity ecosystems of the Appalachian Mountains have a nearly unlimited capacity to surprise. The great mismatch between our limited ability to study them, and the urgency for understanding their rapid change, was brought home to me in June 1995 when John Flynn had arranged for two senior forest pathologists, Phil Wargo and Dave Houston, from the U.S. Forest Service laboratory in Connecticut, to visit sites in southern West Virginia. The visitors had years of experience with forest diseases and insects throughout Pennsylvania, New York, and the Northeast, but little in West Virginia. Upon arrival, they told us of all the stressors they found affecting eastern forests: repeated episodes of logging and burning, subsequent high grading, easy dispersal of even slow-moving species (like the gypsy moth) along highways, livestock and other land-use effects, periodic flareups of native diseases, droughts, and invasions of exotic insects and diseases. It was possible that air pollutants could have an effect, they said, but with all the other variables, it would be hard to detect this effect experimentally, even over decades.

Then we went to the field, climbing quickly through recent pastures and nineteenth-century clearings (now second-growth successional forests), and through a zone that had been logged in the early decades of this century, up to the old growth. There, on the fresh upper slopes and in the high coves, we saw no evidence of recent fires, or high grading, or pasturing of cattle. Neither were there migrant exotics, such as gypsy moth, beech scale, and hemlock adelgid, scourges to the north. None of the stressors the visitors were accustomed to seeing were present, and the forest looked verdant—except for the dead and downed trees. We had been in the field nearly two days before we noticed so much as a mosquito. We were all asking the question everyone asks in the tropics: could the great diversity of tree species in this relatively intact ecosystem be helping to resist the invasions of exotics so generally present in the simpler, much-manipulated forests to the north? Should not an intact, high-diversity ecosystem be the object of intensive study *before* major degradation takes place, not after?

Our special focus for the meeting was an unusual root condition on tulip poplar, first noticed by Joe Aliff, a local landowner. This species is often the dominant in the mixed mesophytic forest, the tallest, the

UV-B damage on tulip poplar leaves

straightest, and the largest in diameter (up to 6 feet), but only rarely exceeding 200 years in age. As it is the most important commercial species these days (since much of the white oak has been removed), any disease in tulip poplar is a concern. An examination of two large tulip poplars turned out by the roots told us only that there was serious root decay. Examination of younger tulip poplars, with the most subtle of basal burling, showed a previously unknown disease condition in the bark of the largest roots. It was not evidently associated with any insect attack, nor with any known pathogen such as shoelace fungus, but the bark of the roots was being pitted down to the wood, an easy pathway for infection of roots by known pathogens. The specialists could suggest no agent for such damage, but they would look further. Tulip poplar was recognized as one of the more ozone-sensitive species. Could the loss of carbohydrate available to roots, due to oxidation by ozone, have allowed a previously unknown agent to affect still another component of this ancient forest?

I thought about all the other species that we knew had begun to die off in these mountains: red mulberry in the early 1960s, chinquapin chestnut; butternut and black oaks in the 1970s; and yellow locust, sassafras, hickories, walnut, the white oaks, beech, yellow buckeye, white basswood, dogwood, hemlock, and sugar maple in the 1980s. Once the previously most disease-resistant species, tulip poplar now appeared to be at risk. We all knew how much research would be needed to unambiguously answer questions as to the cause of change in tulip poplar health, or the changes in any of the other species. It was not just that our ignorance of this complex system was humbling; we lacked an appropriate methodology even to ask the right questions in forests of such biological diversity. The conventional method of growing seedlings of each species separately, exposing them to one or two stressors at a time, and then trying to project the outcome to mature trees, one species at a time, could only be described as primitive.

I was reminded in clear images of the healthy old-growth forests I had grown up with, and the mortality they began to experience in the 1980s. I was reminded as well of the soft green and yellow Carolina parakeet, the only parrot to inhabit eastern North America, described by Audubon as once being present in flocks in the upper canopy of these tall, broadleaf forests. Extinct since 1909, it is hardly remembered and certainly not understood. With that extinction, we lost the potential ever to know what species of tree seeds it helped disperse, or, for that matter, how the evolution of this important consumer would have made sense for us of all the berrylike tree fruits in the Appalachian forests.

Now almost a century later, not only are birds, mammals, and soil insects at risk, even the tree species and ecosystems are at risk. With much more research we might understand the causal agents precisely involved, and, based on that, might propose measures to restore integrity and healthy function to the systems at risk. We do have compelling scientific evidence already. A decision to act now on that evidence seems mainly a matter of whether to care about posterity, as my great-grandfather cared more than a century ago. His was a personal decision, you say, and more compelling science is needed today to persuade us moderns. An essentially conservative view, however, flows from how we value the modern parakeet, the forest of the eastern mountains, and whether we see it as warranting care and prudence, given what we know. Several generations of experience and research clearly indicate prudence, now.

The Broken Web of Life

Sometimes, when we are by ourselves in the deep woods, we think of the forest as a "lonely" place. Actually, it is anything but. In all the woodlands of the Appalachians, in their great variety, myriad creatures are busy taking a living from sunlight and water; from the elements in the soils; from fungi, plants, and trees; and from one another deep beneath the forest duff in the valleys upward to the tops of the tallest spruces on the ridges. This is a busy place of interdependent communities that are the constituents of a web of life whose complexity is beyond the human mind to comprehend.

When we break the strands of this web—through inadvertence or ignorance or (all too often) careless avarice—we break other strands with it, sometimes tearing out whole sections. In the normal course of events, such *disturbances*, as ecologists call them, bring compensating mechanisms into play. The sunlight finds new, unshaded soil. Water increases here and decreases there. New creatures find new niches, and after a time all is well again. However, when the disturbances come too quickly, or are too intense, or too widespread, then the mechanisms of reordering the web of life break down. And that is what is happening in the Appalachians. Through forest clearing; through blights and plagues; through the depletion of nutrients by air pollution and the introduction of toxic chemicals in the air, rain, fog, snow, and ice; through changes in the basic climate itself; the forest's web of life breaks and cannot be mended. It becomes *simplified*, increasingly vulnerable, and in the end loses its ecological viability.

One might suppose that somewhere there is a final strand that must not be broken. If that is true, what are the strand's constituent species? Could they be the most visible of them—the charismatic fauna, as some call them—eagles or bears, let us say, or the cruising trout in the river riffles? Probably not. More likely the final strand supports creatures of a more modest, yet *foundational* attribute. The earthworm and its neighborhood, let us say. Or a wholly invisible family of microorganisms in the soil. Perhaps a wasp, or a species not

Caney Creek waterfall, with mountain laurel, Bankhead National Forest, Alabama

yet fully understood. A water-strider. A fungus that encases feeder roots in a spongelike material, helping them to take up water and nutrients. A certain grass that is needed by a certain insect that is needed by a certain sparrow that is needed... and so forth.

Some attach a kind of religious significance to these interconnections. It is not wrong to have a spiritual sense of the continuing dynamic of nature, for in the 4.5- billion-year history of the planet, and the 15-billion-year history of the cosmos, we are witness to a great mystery still unfolding.

It is this sense of natural mystery, and of the wrongful interruption of its processes, that you should keep in mind as you consider the images and captions that follow and as you read Chris Bolgiano's concluding essay. There you will learn something about the importance of salamanders, the necessity of belonging, and the fate of the web of life in the wondrous forests of the Appalachians.

A fallen tree functions as a nurse log at Heart's Content, Allegheny National Forest, Pennsylvania

The Delicate Balances of Water

Patterning the forested landscape of the Appalachians are the rivers, streams, brooks, forks, runs, and branches that drain a watershed, a watershed being nature's way of subdividing larger geological areas. The soils and the waters defining such places spatially also define them in terms of the plant and animal communities that make up an ecosystem.

The community of creatures that depend on surface water, or at least the moist places associated with it, becomes adapted to the chemicals that are intro-

duced by the drainage of rainfall running over the surface of surrounding soils or seeping down through it. In a stable, undisturbed, and unpolluted ecosystem, the soils tend to neutralize the rainfall, which is normally slightly acidic, before it enters the surface water systems. But today the acidity of rain falling on Appalachian woodlands, such as those drained by brooks, as depicted on these pages, is anything but normal. Should the pH level of the water drop— as it often does in these days of acid deposition—the result could be a hundredfold

A mountain pool along Roaring Fork, Great Smoky Mountains National Park, Tennessee

increase in acidity. In these cases, especially during a heavy rain, even the most well-buffered forest soils cannot raise the pH high enough to keep the waters healthy.

The impacts of this failure can be dramatic. In the unneutralized waters, amphibians and fish—dace, chum, trout—disappear, as do insects that they feed upon. And in time, as has happened from the Adirondacks to the Blue Ridge, streams, ponds, and lakes, even though surrounded by green shrubs and trees, become aquatically unproductive.

Top, blue dasher dragonfly

Above, red-cheeked salamander

Left, fishing spider with dace

Pollution's Rainbow

Facing page, a waterfall near Camp McDowell, Alabama

St. Mary's River, George Washington National Forest, Virginia

Rocks along a brook in Linn State Park, Pennsylvania

This array of photographs shows the effects of two types of pollution. In the most vivid—the orange waterfall and the green pond—the cause is strip mining. In the case of the green holding pond, the mine is active. The orange waterfall effect has been created by an abandoned mine. Once a mining operation is completed, the owners sometimes declare bankruptcy in order to avoid the cost of restoring the stripped site as required by surface mining laws. As a result, the holding ponds break down, sending toxic chemicals into formerly healthy streams.

Ironically, it is the least vivid of these photographs that suggests the most serious effects from pollutants. The waters of St. Mary's River (the slightly orange cast of the rocks is from the minerals they contain, not pollution) are wonderfully clear, but ecologically dead as a result of excess acidity transported long distances on prevailing winds from the factories and power plants of the American midlands.

The streamside rocks with the whitish tinge indicate the presence of aluminum that has been carried into the stream water from the surrounding forest. This metal occurs naturally in virtually all forest soils, but it is "bound up" in silicates. Given enough acid deposition, however, the silicates are broken down, and the free aluminum, which is highly toxic to trees, can be taken up by tree roots. The aluminum, toxic to fish as well, also washes down into streams, leaving the telltale deposits on the rocks. Where this is found, it is likely that the surrounding forest is seriously weakened by air pollution and that the fish are gone.

A holding pond near Cheshire City, Ohio

Beneath the Leaves of Autumn

When you see a patch of maple leaves as lovely as this one, dig down through it. How thick is it? How much decomposition has taken place? Can you find earthworm castings between the leafmold and the soil? Are the older leaves lacy, with the soft tissue eaten by insects, or still intact? When the leaves are as untouched as these, what may very well lie beneath them is a kind of desert where the untidy business of soil-making has come to a standstill.

All manner of creatures—from night-crawlers to termites to centipedes to micro-organisms undetectable by the human eye—

Maple leaves on the forest floor, Ohiopyle State Park, Pennsylvania

live in the upper layers of soil, performing a great service to the forest by converting the fallen leaves, branches, and even the huge trunks of downwood into rich humus. The humus-makers, in turn, support another layer of creatures—salamanders, frogs, and toads. Which, in turn, support other layers in the food chains that make forests like these such a wonder of complexity.

But when the acid rain comes, the chains are broken, the complexity simpli-fied. In many places, the earthworms can no longer be found. Indeed, earthworm populations have decreased by as much as 90 percent in large areas of the Appalachians. The microorganisms die, the beneficial fungi disappear, the amphibians are gone. The woods seem too quiet, too still.

Top, wood frog *Above*, a centipede in leaf litter at Mt. Rogers National Recreation Area, Virginia

Forest scene, showing a range of plant and tree species, Cold Springs Natural Area, Alabama

Brambles beneath dead maples at Mt. Rogers National Recreation Area, Virginia

White-tailed deer, Shenandoah National Park, Virginia

Sunlight in the Shaded Forest

Sunlight, of course, makes plants grow, which is usually beneficial. In a forest such as Cold Springs Natural Area at the left, when a tree dies in the normal course of events, a small patch of woodland receives new light so that seedlings can take the place of the fallen tree. The downed tree itself provides a purchase for more plants and a home for creatures that help it decompose to enrich the soil.

But what happens when forest trees are so weakened by air pollution that large patches of forest trees die? On Mt. Rogers, brambles have grown up where once large maples grew. In other deciduous woodlands, the death of trees in patches, as in the Laurel Mountains shown here, can let in so much light that thick mats of fern make it impossible for seeds to germinate and therefore the forest cannot renew itself. In such areas, forest regeneration is also impeded by deer, which do not like fern, but thoroughly browse off the few tree saplings, shrubs, and other plants that are able to grow in fern-free areas. This has led to the convenient explanation by those wishing to minimize air pollution effects that *deer* are the problem. They're a problem sure enough, but not an excuse for the air pollution that leads to the death of the trees in the first place.

Hayscented fern, Laurel Summit, Forbes State Forest, Pennsylvania

The Forest Banquet's Uninvited Guest

Facing page, Blackberries showing pollution damage near St. Mary's River, George Washington National Forest, Virginia

The plants shown on these pages are all extremely sensitive to damage from ground-level ozone, which damages the leaves it touches by oxidizing the contents. As the ability of the plant to retain its stored carbo-hydrate is decreased, fruiting and flowering are decreased as well. The effect may be clearly seen on the blackberry, favored by black bears and raccoons. Many other food-producing plants are damaged as well—even poison ivy, which itself is part of the food chain despite its unwelcome appear-ance in suburban backyards.

Ozone, the uninvited intruder, does not need to reach levels harmful to humans to have a disastrous impact on forest plants and trees, and therefore wildlife. Over a long enough period of time, even modest levels of ozone can decisively alter the delicate inter-connections of highly adapted species and their food base in the Appalachian forests.

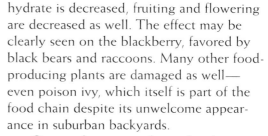

Black-throated green warbler posing on poison ivy

Ozone-damaged poison ivy leaves

Raccoon, Great Smoky Mountains National Park, Tennessee

Butterfly on common milkweed, Shenandoah National Park, Virginia

Facing page, a red oak in Rock Creek Hollow, West Virginia

Top, yellow buckeyes, and (*left*) a pile of white oak acorns on the ground at Laurel Hill State Park, Pennsylvania

Below, gray squirrel at Grandfather Mountain, North Carolina

The Story of Mast

"Mast" is the collective term forest ecologists use for all the different kinds of nuts from woodland trees that accumulate on the ground and are used for food by the creatures of the forest.

Before the chestnut blight, which began at the turn of the century and all but eliminated the tree by the mid-1930s, the American chestnut provided the bulk of mast for squirrels, bears, and other mammals, as well as some birds. In some places the chestnut provided half or more of the forest cover. Its loss was lamentable. Soon, however, oaks in great variety moved in to take the places of the chestnuts, and nutritious, fatty acorns provided a suitable substitute. Other trees producing mast for forest animals include the hickories, beeches, walnuts, the chestnutlike buckeyes and chinquapins, among others.

By any measure, Appalachian mast should be bountiful, even without the chestnut. However, such is not the case. As the impacts of air pollution have taken their toll on the health of the forest over the years, mast production has steadily decreased. In some areas it is down by between 50 and 80 percent. This not only reduces the food supply for mast-dependent animals, but also greatly reduces the regeneration of mast-producing trees, allowing other trees and plants, which are not food sources for species such as squirrels and bears, to take their place.

Black bear at Great Smoky Mountains National Park, Tennessee

A Few Good Woods

In a few good woods things are as they should be, or nearly so. They are, as Chris Bolgiano makes plain in the following essay, *communities*. Notice how the woods depicted on these pages seem to invite the viewer to walk into them. The trees are well spaced, of different ages, unlike a place that has been clearcut. The understory suggests regeneration, and the green plants peeping through the leaves promise a relatively healthy soil. Here, somehow, the forest soils are buffered enough, protected enough, from acid deposition and other airborne attacks to maintain the look and feel of the kind of woodlands that used to be everywhere in the Appalachians. In the photograph, the creatures are hidden, but one senses their presence—some beneath the leaves, others at the tops of trees, and yet more at distance, frightened away by the photographer or perhaps just sleeping. The only things absent here are the very large trees that once greeted newcomers, American Indian and European migrants alike.

It is a pity that there are so few such places left in the Appalachian forests, and that even those are now in peril. We should never forget what a good woods really looks like. Perhaps one day many generations hence they will all look like this. Or perhaps none will.

Deciduous woodlands, Great Smoky Mountains National Park, Tennessee

Communities in Crisis

By Chris Bolgiano

Long associated with the clammy clutter in the pockets of small boys, salamanders are hard to glamorize. They do, after all, live under rocks. They have names like "slimy" and "shovelnose" for reasons entirely deserved. They are unlikely teachers of the meaning of community.

I discovered salamanders when I moved to the hundred acres of central Appalachian woodland where I've lived now for more than a decade. I've spent my entire adult life in Appalachia, but I'll always be an outsider. I am unanchored by ancestry here, rooted only by my longing to belong. It is to the woods that I feel most bound. I walk through them slowly, lifting up rocks, turning over logs, gently parting fern curtains along streambanks. In this way I have found the Jefferson salamander, the slimy, the red, the redback, the dusky, and others that I cannot name. I think of them when the rains come down.

Like a bridge, the slender, curving bodies of salamanders link the two forest worlds of land and water. Like a bridge, they are vulnerable to assault from either side. Emerging from hidden places on wet days in spring or summer, salamanders lay eggs in temporary ponds or along streams or in soggy, rotting tree stumps. They spend their lives in leaf litter or underground, moving around a territory of only a few square yards of forest floor. Although salamanders exist around the world, it's only in the moist, unglaciated Appalachians that they've had time enough and the right conditions to develop the most diverse family of their kind on the planet. Unique species are spread throughout the various Appalachian ranges, but there is a distinct concentration toward the south, with its warmer, wetter climate. All salamanders share the same exquisite form: long, delicate toes, elegantly tapering tail, and scaleless, shining skin through which they breathe.

At only a few grams each, salamanders in aggregate form the weightiest citizen in the woods. They are the most common land-dwelling vertebrate in much of the Appalachians, their biomass exceeding that of all birds and mammals combined. They are the top predators of the leaf litter community, consuming snails, slugs, spiders, beetles, worms, millipedes, and anything else they can wrestle their jaws around. They concentrate fats and nutrients in their tails, and their tissues are exceptionally high in protein. In turn, salamanders provide a valuable food for wild turkeys, snakes, shrews, crows, blue jays, raccoons, possums, and skunks.

To lose salamanders would be to pauperize the entire forest community. But amphibians all over the world are declining, and the few studies done in the Appalachians offer little hope that things are different here. Jefferson salamanders are reported missing from large parts of their range in central Pennsylvania, driven away or killed because of the increasing acidity of the ponds they migrate to in spring. The

Rose River waterfall, Shenandoah National Park, Virginia

ranges of eleven salamander and frog species in south-central New York are shrinking in response to spreading areas of low soil pH. When salamanders lay eggs in water that is low in pH, the embryos tend to curl much more tightly than normal. Few hatch, and those larvae that survive are usually deformed and often killed by loss of body salts drawn out by acidity.

"Habitat loss is still the primary cause of amphibian decline in the Appalachians," according to Joe Mitchell, co-chair (with David Withers of Tennessee) of the Appalachian Working Group of an international task force on declining amphibian populations. "But air pollution, specifically acid precipitation, poses serious threats in some areas." I met Joe years ago when I sought a salamander mentor. Until he donated most of his specimens to the Smithsonian and Carnegie museums, his basement lab at the University of Richmond was lined with gallon jars of pickled snakes and toads, like a well-stocked root cellar. As the leading herpetologist in Virginia, Joe has done field work throughout the region, but in the last few years has concentrated his time in the Appalachians, including Shenandoah National Park. On clear days, from the highest point on my property, I can just see the peak of the park's Hawksbill Mountain 40 miles to the east.

The park receives the highest rates of acid deposition of any national park in the country. It comes from coal-burning power plants from the Great Lakes to the Gulf of Mexico, and from automobile exhaust and industrial smokestacks throughout the region. "The pH of precipitation in the park has been measured as low as 3.0, somewhere below the pH of vinegar," Joe told me. "We know now that heavy precipitation events can cause a short-term lowering of pH. If these pulses occur during egg or larval stages, chances of survival for any one individual are reduced. Several such events could potentially extirpate a local population. Unfortunately, there's just too little research underway to say much about salamander losses. Much more work has been done on fish."

Except for localized use as bait, salamanders have no economic value. Fish, on the other hand, support recreational and commercial businesses. It was fish—or the lack of them—that served as the first red flag of acid rain in America, and it went up in the Adirondacks as early as the 1940s, when declines in lake trout were noted in Big Moose Lake. By the late 1970s, a link between acidic deposition and acidification of lakes was established. Fish communities in Adirondack waters have subsequently been more extensively studied than in any other region.

The Adirondacks are mostly granitic gneisses and metasedimentary rocks. These weather slowly, and the soils derived from them and from the glacial till characteristic of the area are naturally acidic, with little acid-neutralizing capacity. Many lakes were created by the glaciers. Rain and runoff are abundant. So are airborne pollutants. Nearly half of forty high-elevation lakes that had fish in the 1930s have lost them due to rapidly falling pH since then. At higher elevations rain and fog are more frequent and soils are thinner, factors that increase the risk of acidification. A total of one quarter of nearly 1,500 famously beautiful Adirondack lakes are now fishless. All of them are more acidic than lakes that still have fish.

In fact, the soils in the central and southern Appalachians where I live receive as much as or more pollutants than the Adirondacks, but because they weren't scraped away by glaciers, the soils are much deeper. The more soil there is, the more sulfate and nitrate it can soak up, keeping acid from passing into streams. The bedrock of the southern half of the Appalachian region also generally contains more calcium carbonate, giving it more neutralizing capability. These characteristics, we assumed, would protect our prized trout streams, those headwater creeks with moss-covered boulders and rushing water so white and innocent it makes your heart ache. But the assumption was turned on its head in 1987 by 150 volunteers in Virginia. Trained in stream sampling protocol by University of Virginia researchers, and equipped with topographic maps, water bottles, gloves, tags, coolers, and data sheets, the volunteers collected samples from 350 native trout streams in 31 counties. Academic analysts found "greater than expected sensitivity...given the level of acid deposition in the region, it is probable that alkalinity and pH have been reduced in many of these streams." While industry lobbyists and politicians dither over one more study, buffering capacity is being used up.

The findings confirmed what Dr. James Galloway of the University of Virginia was just then concluding after nearly a decade of monitoring water chemistry in fourteen Shenandoah National Park watersheds. Buffering capacity was finite, Galloway found, and provided only a temporary delay of the full effects of acidification. There was "a poor prognosis for aquatic ecosystems in large areas of Shenandoah National Park due to a combination of watershed sensitivity and elevated acidic deposition." When results of the survey carried out by the volunteers came in, Galloway and his research team predicted that at 1990 levels of pollution, one third to nearly all of Virginia's native trout streams would become acidified over the next 30 to 50 years.

Native brook trout are the park's only harvestable resource, and make for a popular fishery. Brookies typically decline as pH drops. As with salamanders, young trout are most vulnerable; egg and fry survival is poorest in streams with the least buffering capacity, and reproduction generally fails below a pH of 4.7. There may be old trout in such streams, but few young ones. Blacknose dace, a small native fish on which trout sometimes prey, show stunted growth in streams with low pH. In laboratory experiments, dace and brook char swam strongly away from water channels with a pH lower than 5.1.

In the real world, when fish can't swim away they die: pulses of acid rain from storms or snowmelt are continuously causing fish kills across the Appalachians. In Pennsylvania, nearly two dozen streams and lakes have been removed from stocking programs because so few fish survive. Virginia's stocking program has experienced at least three fish kills from acidification in the past 5 years. The Cherokee Trout Hatchery on the Cherokee Reservation in North Carolina lost 40,000 pounds of fish from a single flush of acidified flood waters from Raven Fork in the Great Smoky Mountains National Park. The kills started in 1981, and pulses of water with a pH of 4.0 still rush in when fronts come out of the west with more than 2 inches of rain. Now the water is artificially buffered with sodium hydroxide before it reaches the fish.

Sporadic catastrophes draw sporadic attention, but gradual, cumulative, more profoundly threatening changes often go unnoticed. Indeed, it's hard to grasp how radically the world of seldom-seen creatures has already been altered without some knowledge of its structure before change began. For that you need historical data, which are rare. Just a few miles south of Shenandoah National Park, in the George Washington National Forest, the St. Mary's River has been monitored for more than half a century. St. Mary's River Wilderness Area, famous for trout and waterfalls, provides one of the only reliable long-term records of changes in an Appalachian aquatic community.

It was very nearly the shortest day of the year when I hiked up St. Mary's with Larry Mohn, and even at noon the sun hung low over Big

Spy Mountain. We passed in and out of shadows that changed the complexion of the forest from bright and glittery to dim and solemn. As we followed the stream along its canyon of fractured cliffs and talus slopes, Larry pointed out his sampling sites. A biologist for the Virginia Department of Game and Inland Fisheries, he's been surveying the aquatic life of St. Mary's River every 2 years since 1986. Larry did his first surveys there in 1976, and his tallies can be statistically compared with baseline data collected by biologist Eugene Surber as early as 1936.

"The wild, reproducing population of rainbow trout that Surber observed in 1936 disappeared by 1994," said Larry. We were standing beside a deep pool where cold, thin sunlight turned the water glassy-eyed, as in death. The loss of rainbows brought the number of extirpated fish species in St. Mary's to six, half of the original total of twelve. "Then last year's unusually wet winter badly hurt the native brook trout that moved downstream to reclaim their old range from the rainbows, which were introduced long ago," Larry continued. "I wouldn't be surprised if the heavy rainstorm at the end of January '96 took the water pH down to 4.0." Brook trout eggs hatch around mid-January. The St. Mary's River population declined more than 70 percent, with almost no reproduction.

During that time span, the pH fell from 7.0 to an average of around 5.0. Like Shenandoah National Park, St. Mary's has been protected for decades from human manipulation, and the possibility of lingering influences from earlier land uses was investigated and discounted. Air pollution is the sole remaining culprit.

There were occasional sandy beaches along the St. Mary's that would have made for good tracking, but the stream was high on the day of my visit and had washed away any scratchings of small feet. But whoever depends on the river for food is surely hurting. Mammals that eat fish, like the mahogany curve of a mink I once glimpsed from my downstairs window, and the otters that have been reintroduced in parts of the southern Appalachians, are locally at risk for starvation. So is an uncommon species of water shrew (*Sorex palustris punctulatus*) in the Smokies and Alleghenies. Fish-eating birds have been forced to abandon waters where acidification has killed off their prey. Swallows and flycatchers, which feed on emerging aquatic insects, must feel the pinch too. My heart sinks to think of the Louisiana waterthrush that returns each year to nest beside one of my creeks, and whose cascading call ushers in spring.

One of the characteristics of my woodlot is its shallow, shaley soil. Comes a big wind, and at least a few trees go down every time, ripping roots out of the ground. In winter snow I have followed gray fox tracks down into a pit left by roots. I guess it must have been a relatively warm place to spend a night. In summer I've watched dirt in the root balls of newly downed trees dribble away like blood. The pit and mound topography formed by blowdowns is characteristic of Appalachian forests. It allows mineral soils to mix with decaying leaf litter, enriching the soil-building process. It also gives me a view of the soil striations that, with weather patterns, shape the character of my land.

Soils are the foundation of the forest's architecture of living forms. As a forest stand matures, its soil tends to become naturally more acidic because older trees take up less of the available nitrogen. For a while, this fact added to the confusion over the effects of acid deposition, but there is now widespread acknowledgment that the rate of soil acidification is far greater than any normal process could produce. As soil pH is driven down, the decomposition of leaves and woody debris from which humus is made slows down. The community of soil microbes that consumes and breaks down forest floor litter shifts from bacteria to fungi, some of which are more tolerant of acid conditions. However, one of the most influential groups of fungi, the mycorrhizae, whose symbiotic relationship with root tips makes essential nutrients available to trees, declines with acidification.

Bacteria and fungi form the diet of most worms, and worms that feed mainly on bacteria decline. Woodlice can shrug off fairly heavy doses of a single pollutant, but succumb to the synergistic interaction of several. Populations of other soil invertebrates—mites, springtails, tardigrades, rotifers—shift toward species already adapted to acidic soils. In some studies the total number of soil organisms remained roughly the same, as members of a few acid-tolerant species increased to fill the vacancies left by more sensitive species. In every study, the total number of species always declined.

There's been little research in the United States on the effects of air pollution on larger wildlife, but Canadian and European scientists are assembling an impressive body of evidence. Rarely is the impact direct and attributable, like the death of hundreds of songbirds near a pulp mill in British Columbia from hemorrhaging in lungs and livers after inhaling hydrogen sulfide. Or of owls, songbirds, bats, and small mammals from the same pollutant in the vicinity of oil wells. More common are insidious, unnoticed effects from widespread, chronic, sublethal doses. These start in the soil.

The chemical wash of airborne pollutants leaches out plant nutrients like calcium and magnesium and activates formerly dormant toxins, especially aluminum. So the browse that my local Bambi family munches annually along the edges of the butterfly meadow becomes not only depleted but poisoned. Two fawns were born last spring somewhere close to the house, though they and their mother only occasionally show themselves. Maybe one of them grew a set of spikes, or a strange buck entered the neighborhood, because in the fall I noticed peeled saplings where a deer had rubbed his itching head. But how healthy might the new spikes be? In an industrial area of Poland, the antlers of roe deer (the European equivalent of my whitetails) were collected from before 1920 to 1973 and compared. By the late 1950s they had deteriorated drastically, reflecting the impact on forage of emissions from a nearby steel mill.

In Canada, studies suggest that sulfates in forest forage disturb enzymatic and other metabolic functions in herbivores. Blacktailed deer in Washington State that browsed on plants doused with fluoride from a nearby aluminum plant showed severe dental disfigurement and abnormal thickening in long bones. Fluoride was found not only in bones of deer but also in cottontail rabbits, hares, muskrats, ground squirrels, woodchucks, deer mice, voles, and house sparrows, and in carnivores such as red foxes and barn owls.

The draining away of calcium has special consequences for birds, in effect a reprise of the DDT phenomenon in which eggshells became too thin to function. A study in Sweden found that aluminum mobilized in soil contaminated the insects eaten by flycatchers, which caused a calcium deficiency in the birds' eggs. In The Netherlands, the reduction of soil calcium caused by aluminum resulted in lower amounts of calcium in tree leaves, then in the caterpillars that ate the leaves, and then in the birds that ate the caterpillars, again resulting in thin-shelled eggs.

Aluminum and some trace metals are naturally present in soil but generally remain inert until activated by the chemistry of acid rain. Other heavy metals are deposited from the air. Metal accumulation through the food chain has been extensively documented. Arsenic emissions in a German forest in 1936 killed red and roe deer and rabbits. Cadmium has been found in tissues of sparrowhawks and song thrushes near a smelter in England, in wild rabbits near a smelter in Montana, and in moose in Canada and Maine along a gradient associated with industrial air pollution. Moose and deer have been found with enough cadmium in their livers and kidneys to threaten any humans that eat them.

Mercury is known to accumulate at the top of aquatic food chains. The first documented case of mercury poisoning in a wild mammal was a female mink found near the South Saskatchewan River in 1975. Researchers in the northeastern United States found mercury-caused lesions on the central nervous systems of 44 percent of the wild mink studied. Otters in a Wisconsin river watershed had the highest tissue levels of mercury of any the furbearers analyzed, followed by mink, raccoon, fox, muskrat, and beaver. The fur of mink and otter from the industrialized part of the watershed was higher in mercury than in those from other areas.

Chronic mercury poisoning results in gradual incapacitation. Endangered Florida panthers, their total population hovering around fifty, have died from mercury poisoning after eating raccoons whose diet was largely aquatic. Other panthers are suspected of being prone to getting hit by cars because mercury has dulled their coordination and hearing. Mercury poisoning of wildlife may be a widely unrecognized phenomenon, because the evidence—animals with poor judgment—is not easily detected.

After years in Appalachia, I'm still discovering forest communities I've never noticed before—in tree holes, on rocks in the spray zone of waterfalls, in the fissured bark of old trees. The diversity of lichens that live on the bark of mature trees is another characteristic of the Appalachians. Some of them are extremely sensitive to sulfur dioxide. Parula warblers, one of the neotropical migratory birds that flash like jewels in the Appalachian canopy each spring and fall, are declining in northern areas where a particular pollution-sensitive lichen is no longer available to supply nesting material. Lichens are important foods for other species, notably caribou in the north, but also some smaller animals like voles.

Foods of many other kinds are being seriously depleted. The severity of the anthracnose fungus that has completely eradicated flowering dogwood trees from some parts of the Appalachians is strongly linked to acid deposition. Dogwood blossoms form a pearly necklace at the forest's throat each spring; their berries feed dozens of species, especially migratory birds. Dogwood browse is preferred by herbivores large and small. Air pollution is also a suspect in the mysterious oak wilt that threatens the abundance of acorns, in many areas the single most important winter food for bears, deer, wild turkey, and squirrels. Insects and diseases that attack plants are by nature adapted to take advantage of trees under stress, and benefit greatly from the weakening of trees by air pollution.

Even more detrimental to plants than acid deposition is ozone in the lower atmosphere. Formed from reactions of hydrocarbons and nitrogen oxides in the presence of sunlight, ozone is a gas taken in by plant leaves. Damage is often clearly visible—red, brown, or purple stippling between veins on upper leaf surfaces, and leaves dropped too early in the fall. The result is reduced photosynthesis and plant growth, especially of seedlings. Ozone can also reduce pollen germination and flower and cone production in trees. At higher elevations, ozone concentrations don't decrease at night as they do in the lowlands. Many early successional trees such as big-toothed aspen and white ash open their leaf stomata around dawn, earlier than late successional trees, and are more vulnerable to ozone. Trees that show ozone injury are attacked more often by destructive insects. The danger is not only that individual trees will produce less food, but that plants sensitive to ozone will gradually be outcompeted by those that are resistant. Communities that rely on those plants for food or habitat will be diminished.

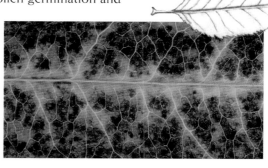

Ozone damage to black cherry tree leaf

Researchers in Great Smoky Mountains and Shenandoah national parks have found 95 plant species affected by ozone, among them some of the most important to wildlife and human beings: blackberry, sassafras, yellow poplar, yellow birch, red maple, sugar maple, sweetgum. By far the most sensitive plants are black cherry trees and several species of milkweed. From the goings-on in my butterfly meadow I can testify to the nursery role of milkweed for monarchs. What really dominates the meadow, though, is a lone black cherry tree. Every August the pileated woodpeckers shriek with laughter like crazy women to find it laden with fruit. Chipmunks slide down drooping branches, stuffing their cheeks. Raccoons climb up at night. Most of the cherries are gone by heavy frost, to be finished off by late flocks of cedar waxwings.

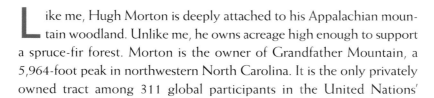

L ike me, Hugh Morton is deeply attached to his Appalachian mountain woodland. Unlike me, he owns acreage high enough to support a spruce-fir forest. Morton is the owner of Grandfather Mountain, a 5,964-foot peak in northwestern North Carolina. It is the only privately owned tract among 311 global participants in the United Nations'

Biosphere Reserve Program. Hugh Morton has white eyebrows that brim over his glasses and a heavy fringe of white hair around a bald pate. He is of comfortable girth and kindly mein. He looks…well, grandfatherly. His role as land protector, though, dates back at least to 1952, when he inherited 4,000 acres on Grandfather Mountain. In past years he has struggled to balance the demands of tourism and development with conservation of Grandfather's many rare species. These days, it is the spruce-fir forest that causes him the most anguish.

The red spruce and Fraser fir forests of the southern Appalachians are the last exhalations of the glaciers' icy breath. The dark, coniferous north woods retreated far southward in response to cold from the Laurentide ice sheet. About 18,000 years ago, spruce, pine, and fir covered the Atlantic coastal plain through the Great Plains to the Rocky Mountains. As warming increased, deciduous trees began a slow, quiet infiltration of coniferous communities. Only on the highest peaks of the Appalachians has the spruce-fir ecosystem survived.

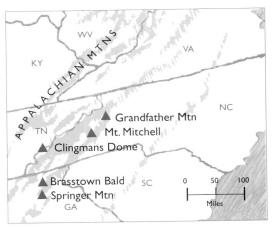

Over the past decade, these dense forests, so dark that the Black Mountains of North Carolina were named for them, have been punched with holes. Dead trunks stand like stick figures amidst the full-fleshed green of still-living trees. That's how it looked to me on MacRae Peak, one of Grandfather Mountain's series of promontories that shape the silhouette of a bearded man lying face up to the sky. There was snow on the ground. Against it, the blue-green fir and yellow-green spruce were easy to trace as they sprinkled ever more sparsely down the slopes. The shriveled red of mountain ash berries gave a rosy glow to the brown screen of bare branches below. Mountains in the distance were a powdery, nostalgic blue tinged with melancholy purple. Mt. Mitchell, at 6,684 feet the highest peak east of the Mississippi, lost its distinct contours against the horizon as haze thickened through the afternoon.

The trail was rooty and rocky. In some places I grappled with knotted cables up rock faces glazed with ice. In others, there were ladders. Along the ridgeline, leaves on rhododendrons were laid flat back with frost like the ears of a frightened animal. Today it was warm, and sun gleamed on the dead white trunks of spruce and fir snags, their branches broken off to stubs. I passed a tag on a tree. Grandfather Mountain is one of the Tennessee Valley Authority's forest monitoring sites, but the high elevation plot was inaugurated too recently to come up yet for re-measuring, which would show changes. Thirty years ago, Hugh Morton began worrying about the number of trees dying. He learned then about the balsam woolly adelgid, an insect introduced from Europe that has by now killed most of the mature Fraser firs in the southern Appalachians. Fifteen years ago he saw that the red spruce was not affected by the adelgid, but it was also dying.

Nearly half of all red spruce trees at high elevations, from the Green and White mountains of New England, through the Adirondacks of New York, to the Blue Ridge, Balsams, and Smokies of the South, have died in the past 15 years. Surveys in the southern Appalachians show that growth rates of both spruce and fir began to slow markedly in the

1960s. West-facing slopes appear to have a higher rate of decline. Drought, ice storms, windthrows, insects—all are blamed, and all play a part in the intricate life of the spruce-fir community. Forest ecosystems are so complex that individual causes and effects are hard to tease out, but the correlation of spruce decline with air pollutants is overwhelming.

The greatest amounts of sulfur and nitrogen received in the Appalachians are concentrated at high elevations, where highly acidic fog hangs day after day, and drips in slow drops from branch tips. Grandfather Mountain's backcountry manager recently measured the pH of rime ice at 4.0. In Great Smoky Mountains National Park, which has the largest remaining chunk of spruce-fir forest, cloud-water acidity has been measured down to a pH of 2.0. Most of the park's high elevation catchments are saturated with nitrogen. Too much nitrogen taken up by spruces prolongs the growing season and interferes with the hardening process against severe cold that is essential. Winter then kills the buds. Unused nitrogen runs off downslope, acidifying lower reaches. The aluminum in the soils has reached toxic levels.

Air pollution is implicated not only in the decline of red spruce, but also in weakening Fraser firs and making them more vulnerable to adelgids in the first place. Polluted spruce forests in Europe have been heavily infested with gall lice, bark beetles, and sawflies. European spruce and fir have also been shown to lose nutrients due to leaching out by ozone.

Rapid loss of trees is the most dramatic impact of air pollution, a sort of demolition of nature's community meetinghouse. Where new species have been discovered in Appalachian spruce-fir forests, it is only in time to record their demise. A new beetle species found in 1981 in three places in the Great Smokies and Balsam mountains could be dependably collected from the moist undersides of fungus-covered sticks and small logs in stands thick with Fraser fir. But by 1993, attempts to find the beetles netted only two individuals. By then the firs were bleached skeletons and the ground beneath them was no longer protected from drying out. The rare bryophytes that lived on the fir trunks were gone too.

A tiny tarantula known as the spruce-fir moss spider, discovered on Mt. Mitchell in 1923, lives only in moist mats of moss growing on rocks and boulders in conifer shade. By 1995, when the spider was officially added to the federal Endangered Species List, the largest and apparently the only reproducing population lived on Grandfather Mountain. A species of rock lichen, which requires the same habitat, has been recommended for the endangered list.

But I find I mourn most the loss of salamanders. Grandfather Mountain is at the center of the limited Blue Ridge range of the Yonahlossee salamander. This is considered the handsomest of the Appalachian salamanders, brick red on top with charcoal gray and ash-flecked sides. I've spent hours looking unsuccessfully under rocks for them on Mt. Rogers in Virginia, their northernmost reach, about a hundred miles south of my place. At home I have redbacks, aptly named and very attractive in their own right, and much more common. Yet they, too, are missing from areas where they should be found but where soil pH has fallen too low. I uncovered a redback not long ago in my garden mulch pile. Unlike lizards and skinks, salamanders do not skitter. Towering over him like the neighborhood bully, I watched as he stepped deliberately away.

A Culture at Risk

Before reading these introductory paragraphs we suggest you take a moment to compare the photographs in the next two picture spreads. In the tension between the first of these and the second lies the Appalachian tragedy, a continuing story of a wanton exploitation of a people and their place.

As the photograph of the young hunter on this page suggests, people live close to nature in the Appalachian highlands, an aspect of the self-sufficiency of the Scots-Irish who settled here in the early eighteenth century. Arriving in the New World and finding the tidewater and piedmont lands already occupied, the doughty pioneers took up residence in the mountains where a mule and single-bottom plow was as much agricultural technology as was needed for the small-field agriculture, the only kind of farming the narrow valleys would allow. Accordingly, the mountain people eked out the agriculture with subsistence hunting and fishing, and the use of wild plants, characteristics of their economy to this day.

They built scattered villages and towns, as shown on the next page, with houses close together in valleys, hollows, and coves. A neighborliness ensued, and a self-reliance that some mistake for distrust of outsiders. In fact, the integration of livelihood with the natural environment and with one's neighbors is an ideal American lifestyle that neither flatland agronomists, factory workers, nor people who wear suits in cities can come close to achieving. The caricature in popular literature and films of a people absorbed with family feuds and moonshining is a perversion of what most of us believe to be admirable qualities: close-knit families and gutsy independence. Indeed, it was in the Appalachians—not Philadelphia—that colonists first declared independence from Great Britain. In northeastern Tennessee, the Watauga Association dissolved the bonds with the Crown and formed their own government in 1772. "They were," as Theodore Roosevelt admiringly described them, "the first men of American birth to estab-

Wesley Scarbro squirrel hunting, Rock Creek, West Virginia

127

lish a free and independent community on the continent."

However hard won, the independence of the people of the Appalachians, most notably in the central and southern areas of the mountains, has been under increasing attack for most of this century from giant multinational corporations and the agencies of government that support them. In the past several decades especially—the decades of pollution—the corporate siege has escalated dramatically. In one of his bitterest moments, the late John Flynn put it this way: "The shrewder, money-minded people," he said, "control the destinies of those whose values are of a higher order. It's forever been that way and forever will be—until the final lump of coal comes out of these valleys and the final tree is cut."

This chapter is about the epic struggle of those that John Flynn described as having values of a higher order, a struggle to maintain their culture and livelihood in the face of the unrelenting compulsion of giant corporations to profit from the destruction of the mountains. The following pages graphically demonstrate the ways the citizens of the Appalachians have been hanging on, in spite of the stripmines and chipping mills of those who worship the bottom line without regard for the God-given beauty of the mountains and their people.

An aerial view of Peachtree Creek, West Virginia

A Tragedy Twice Over

The size of the dragline in this picture is indicated by comparing it with the automobile nearby, which looks like a child's toy. Such a machine, ten stories high with its giant scoop (53 cubic yards), can dismantle mountains, carve valleys, create whole new landforms at a scale that once took the forces of nature thousands of years to bring about.

Now, however, the money men in headquarters offices and government buildings can decide, as they have here, that the coal beneath such a mountain is more important than the mountain itself. More important than its crucial function in the ecosystem of which it is a part. More important than the people who once lived on or near it, or who hunted over it, or simply hiked to the top to take in the view on a summer Sunday.

The devastation is not yet done. The coal so ruthlessly stripped is loaded into railroad cars that crawl westward to be burned in the power plants that then inject their gasses into the atmosphere. Thus are the toxic waste products of the coal returned to the mountains whence they came—in the form of pollution that grievously injures the forests the dragline has yet to destroy.

The law requires that after the coal is gone, the earth movers put the mountain back as best they can. Sometimes the executives of the corporations decide to install a golf course on the former mountaintop, and though this green emblem of privilege is appallingly out of place here, the executives nevertheless boast of their corporate responsibility.

A dragline removes a mountaintop to get at bituminous coal in Cabin Creek, West Virginia

Above, cemetery in the forest on "Graveyard Hill," West Virginia

Relatives, including Daisy Ross (*left*) and Tanners Mollet (*top right*) gather annually to tend the graves

Guardians of the Forest

Curiously, it is in death that mountain people are often most effective in protecting their Appalachian heritage and in asserting their independence from those in the corner-suite offices of multinational corporations.

A provision of the mining law decrees that mining companies cannot carry on operations any closer than 300 feet from a cemetery. Moreover, even though the mining corporations may own the surrounding land, they must nevertheless permit access. In the photos shown here, the cemetery is cared for by descendants of African Americans who once lived in the area. Every year they gather, traveling from distant cities all over the United States, to maintain their family gravesites on this small high-ground sanctuary.

So can the corporations—some of which have turned entire hollows where houses once stood into slurry ponds—be thwarted by little islands of sanity, reverence, and hope.

Cemetery on Montcoal Mountain, West Virginia

Ginseng roots drying in a Naoma, West Virginia, front window

A Confiscated Commons

Joe Williams digging ginseng with a "seng hoe" in Tom's Hollow. The area is now closed off for mining

Below, Ivan Jarrell and Mary Hufford, in the Wills newground on Rock Creek, West Virginia

Traditionally, the wooded mountains have been seen as a "commons" by the Appalachian people, who borrowed from their British forebears the practice that kept areas open to all for proper use, regardless of who had legal title. Among the proper uses is "ginsenging" in the central and southern parts of the range. Ginseng, considered a panacea by Asians, has become a major cash crop. In Kentucky alone more than 50,000 dry pounds of ginseng root are exported every year. And yet, the woods are increasingly being closed off, logged off, stripped off by corporations that can acquire acreage at bargain prices from land-poor local residents. In protest, the Stanley family festival–reunion shown below takes place every year on a patch of mountain land they still own. The state road to this area offers one of the few public views of mountaintop removal by mining operations in the entire state. The company is trying to get the road closed.

Above, a mining company gate bars access to forest land that for generations had been used as a *de facto* commons for hunting, gathering, and recreation

The Stanley family reunion celebrates as well as protects Kayford Mountain by protesting mining company operations with a joyful noise

A Fragile Bounty

Conserves, preserves, jams, and jellies made from fruits gathered in the wild, as well as those grown in garden plots and orchards, are a significant part of Appalachian fare. An unusual wild food found in the central and southern mountains is ramps, a wild leek that is gathered each year for community-wide ramp suppers. Ramps, which are said to be good for the heart, can be fried, eaten with eggs, even pickled.

Among the forest trees yielding fruit for Appalachian tables and small boys are paw-paws, persimmons, and black walnuts. Now missing is the red mulberry. Susceptible to air pollution, this climbable, wide-spreading tree has all but disappeared in the Appalachians.

The butternut is also susceptible to air pollution, especially tropospheric ozone, and has been placed on the endangered species list. The proximate cause of its

A display of Pauline Carnes' canning skill at "Nectars of the Wild," near Clayton, Georgia

demise is a virulent canker discovered in 1967. Experts now believe the butternut, like the chestnut before it, will become lost to the forest. The fruit of this small tree (also known as white walnut) has a sticky pod that produces a brown stain on the fingers—a permanent dye once used for coloring fabrics. The nut itself is wonderfully sweet. In fact, butternut sugar can be made from the sap, though the yield is much less than that of the sugar maple.

Above, Ben Burnside gathering ramps in Rock Creek

Below, butternuts and a dying butternut tree, Rock Creek, West Virginia

The Hardwood Economy

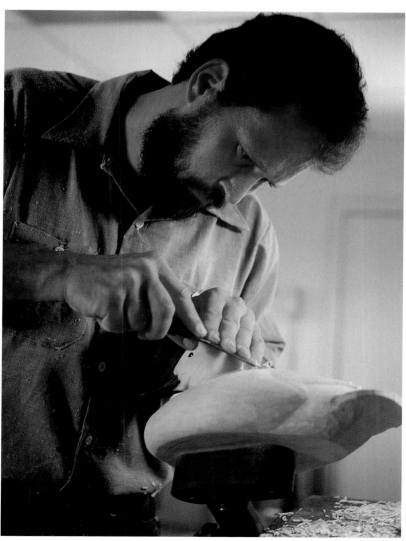

Facing page, a "snapped" maple tree, rotted at the base

Left, Orville Woody puts the finishing touches on an Appalachian ladderback chair in Spruce Pine, North Carolina

Below, Vermont craftsmen making decoys and wooden hats

Wood crafts are a long-time tradition in the Appalachians, with skills handed down through the generations. In recent years, such artistic work has become a stable source of income and employment in small factories and shops in the mountain towns. In addition, the hardwoods of the region are the primary source for the giant furniture and wood fabrication factories located adjacent to the mountains in North Carolina, Virginia, Tennessee, and elsewhere that depend on the arboreal cornucopia provided by the mountains.

Thus air pollution and tree clearing for mining and chipping mills will increasingly affect the hardwood manufacturing and craft economy. For example, the largest fabricator of stairway parts in the United States has found that it can no longer count on a steady supply of beechwood, the best wood for its products, in view of the widespread decline of this tree throughout the Appalachians.

The dead maple shown on the opposite page, rotted from the long-term effects of air pollution, will make no chair or wooden toy or carving board. It stands as a grim reminder that the craft traditions of the mountains are vulnerable.

Fading Foliage

The New England Yankees call them "leaf peepers"—the city people who come to the White Mountains of New Hampshire or the Green Mountains of Vermont or the Adirondacks of upstate New York to be amazed at the fall foliage display. The old-timers mean no disrespect, of course, for leaf peeping is a major part of the economy in large areas of the Appalachians. And as the large photograph on this page amply demonstrates, New England has no corner on vividness.

But as the smaller photograph shows, not every year is a good one. Indeed, some will tell you that the New England autumns seem to be drabber year by year. Is this just

Autumn colors brighten a West Virginia hillside

an imagined result of air pollution? Perhaps not. Recent research at Hubbard Brook in the White Mountains of New Hampshire has conclusively confirmed what scientists have long known (though disputed by apologists for industry and those who wish to confuse the issue): that decades of acid rain have robbed the forest soils of vital nutrients. Alkaline chemicals have been so thoroughly leached from the soil that the forest trees have simply stopped growing. In fact, they haven't grown for 10 years.

The no-growth effect, together with climate change, the impacts of tropospheric ozone, and increasing levels of UV-B radiation put the forests of the Appalachians at risk—along with the culture and the economy they support.

A disappointing season for fall foliage in New Hampshire

The Last of the Hardwood Forests

Throughout the Appalachians, especially in the southern part of the mountains, the old-growth hardwood forests are being cleared—and the logs often sent to chipping mills—so that pine plantations can

Above, an Alabama tree farm

Right, slash after a clearcut, Bankhead National Forest, Alabama

be established to make two-by-fours. Commercial foresters and those who serve them in government would like people to believe that the tree farms are forests too. They are not. A forest is an ecosystem; a tree farm grows lumber as a crop, like corn or soybeans.

And the destruction of these age-old forest ecosystems is permanent. Once leveled, they can never be restored, even if a later generation might think twice about the terrible devastation and waste their forebears brought about merely to pump up prices on the New York Stock Exchange for a year or two with no thought of the consequences—to nature or to the people who once made a living and created a culture in the vanished hardwood forests of the Appalachians.

Keeping the Faith

These old mountains inspire faith, of course, and a belief in better days for each of us. Baptism, such as that practiced here, is an ancient ritual that affirms *belonging*; that one is accepted, not alone, able to draw on the strength of the community in times of travail—an important notion in the Appalachians.

In the early church, immersion in "living" (i.e., running) water was associated with repentance and the renunciation of evil, not simply the naming of infants, which came centuries later. To St. Paul, baptism meant dying in sin and being raised joyously to new life.

The church people of the Appalachians honor these formative traditions in the living waters of their region. They have been sinned against more than they have sinned. Yet they have never given up, nor lost their sense of humor about the tribulations that corporations and governments visit upon them, as Mary Hufford's perceptive essay, beginning on the next page, shows.

Sturdy mountains, and trees and people, are what the Appalachians are all about. And faith. And grace. And hope.

James Dickens and Rev. Larry Brown baptizing Vicky Jarrell in Coal River, West Virginia

Weathering the Storm
Cultural Survival in an Appalachian Valley
by Mary Hufford

The Central Appalachian Plateau, a vast and ancient tableland etched over eons into thousands of winding hollows, spreads away from its center in southern West Virginia and eastern Kentucky south through Tennessee to Alabama and north into Ohio and Pennsylvania. Trickling down from the ridges and welling up from deep springs, waters gather and flow into the tributaries of the great rivers bordering the plateau. Deep indentations known variously as "coves," "drains," and "swags" wrinkle the ridges and slopes rising away from the hollows. Sheltered in these coves against extreme climate change, and nurtured by rich layers of erosional humus, the world's oldest and biologically richest temperate zone hardwood forest has taken shape. The pioneering botanist and forest ecologist E. Lucy Braun, who first perceived it as a coherent system, named it the "mixed mesophytic." Because the mixed mesophytic provided the seed for reforesting the eastern United States as the glaciers ebbed, some ecologists have nicknamed it "the Mother Forest."

The diversity of the mixed mesophytic forest is remarkable. Whereas most forest types are dominated by two or three species, the mixed mesophytic harbors eighty woody species in its canopy and understory. Among them are white basswood, yellow buckeye, tulip poplar, sugar maple, red maple, sweet birch, beech, red, white, and black oaks, all the hickories, four kinds of magnolia, black locust, white and black walnut, chestnut, chinquapin, dogwood, redbud, hazelnut, witch hazel, elm, red mulberry, persimmon, and pawpaw, all of which have for generations been woven into the fabric of community life on the central Appalachian plateau.

This magnificent forest puts on a year-round show. Bristling in winter like the hair on a wild boar's back, studded with the blossoms of dogwoods and redbuds in spring, muted in summer's green mantle, or ablaze with autumn's full spectrum, this forest grabs your attention and doesn't let go. Drive along any of the deep crevices riven by the tributaries of southern West Virginia's Big Coal River, and the immediacy of the forest canopy is unnerving. You do not exactly drive through this forest, you drive at it, for it grows at you from the slopes: directly in your face on the straight stretches, separating to wind you around horseshoe curves. These are the kinds of roads they made "by tossing a snake in the path and following it up the mountain," in the words of the late Mae Bongalis, a respected elder in the town of Naoma.

John Flynn, the science writer who developed the Appalachia Forest Action Project, theorized that the dynamism of this forest whets the appetite for color displayed in the yards and homes of residents. The color modulates with the seasons and reaches its apex at Christmas,

The forks of Peachtree Creek and Drew's Creek, West Virginia

147

during the annual pause in the spectacle of forest and garden. Navigating the roads that wind from Marmet to Naoma, I am distracted by the colors of the yards.

Like the "Bill Dickens" beans Mae Bongalis would string into "leather britches" each fall, Route 3 threads together dozens of hollows and tiny coal camps: Bloomingrose, Prenter, Seth, Orgas, Sylvester, Elk Run, Seng Creek, Whitesville, Leevale, Pax, Eunice, Edwight, Montcoal, Stickney,

Mae Bongalis, of Naoma, stringing beans

Hazy, Pettry Bottom, Sundial, Horse Creek, Naoma, Peachtree, Dry Creek, Rock Creek. The diversity of homes and yard decor rivals the diversity of the forest. Brick dwellings with two-story columns built by retirees share a mountainside with once-mobile homes absorbed within a growing maze of porches, decks, and ells. Log cabins, springhouses, smokehouses, corncribs, and barns—signs of a persistent system of forest farming— are interspersed with structures of every conceivable material: cinderblock, brick, aluminum siding, and latticework.

The landscape continually recreated here is a vigorous pastoral–industrial hybrid. Fence rails and posts may be of wormy chestnut and yellow locust, or they might be of augur shafts and steel cable scavenged from abandoned mines. The top of an old camper may be sheltering potatoes stored underground for the winter, while the "fodder shocks" of bundled corn stalks that originated as vegetable shelters now serve as decorative facades. But the front porches, where people sit and talk, are no facade. They are well-worn seats to the stage of the road and the forested slopes beyond, apt to become stages themselves, for telling the stories that conjure this place.

The human scale of the landscape at eye level is skewed by massive industrial designs. A towering, green embankment stretching between two mountains startles your eye as you round a curve. A corrugated pipe 4 feet in diameter crosses the road 30 feet above your car and disappears into the mountains on both sides. You wait at a railroad crossing as a train crawls by hauling several hundred cars, each laden with a hundred tons of coal. You pass the imposing structures of the A.T. Massey Coal Company: Elk Run, Marfork, Performance, and Goals. At night these glow with the radiance of a thousand tungsten bulbs, maintaining an eerie and defensive presence. Mounted with guards, gates, watchtowers, and the American flag, the operations look and feel like an occupying force.

Even as I keep a wary eye out for the next coal truck flying by enroute to the loading docks on the Kanawha River, the ever-modulating gardens along Route 3 vie for my attention. From window boxes and borders, flowers—from azaleas to zinnias—stage their multicolor riot. Beyond these are the vegetable gardens, trumpeting the rich soils that gave rise to the mixed mesophytic. Large, lush, and neatly laid out, even in the narrow strips between river and road, the gardens burgeon each year with spring lettuce, peas, onions, sweet potatoes, corn, potatoes, beans, cabbages, broccoli, beets, tomatoes, and grapes.

In the fall the gardens are cleared away. Autumn harvest displays begin with late squashes and chrysanthemums. Thereafter, against the backdrop of the early winter forest, the drama escalates, through Halloween to Christmas, with a final display at Easter before the gardens begin again.

In my mind, Christmas deserves to be called the river's fifth season. From Thanksgiving weekend on, the lights begin appearing, like one long fireworks display bursting slowly across the landscape. For those who indulge, every surface seems fair game. Lights and red ribbons outline trees, cyclone fences, rooflines, and satellite dishes. By the dozens, sometimes by the hundreds, figures appear in yards from the mouths of hollows to their most remote heads: stars of David, hovering angels, elves at work, reindeers pulling Santa, and scenes of Bethlehem and Calvary.

As I read it, this visual feast is a celebration of community life, place, and staying power. John Flynn summed it up: "These Christmas lights are audacious!"

In the early 1990s John Flynn came home to Coal River, after 30 years of being away. Like others of his generation, born into the dendritic depressions of the coal-rich plateau as the coal industry mechanized, he joined the Appalachian diaspora flooding the "hillbilly highways" toward the Rust Belt. "We learned that the three R's were "Reading, Writing, and the Road to Akron," John told me. Biographical time for those committed to making Coal River home may include many years spent working elsewhere before coming home to retire.

Flynn, however, was far from retiring. For 2 years before an aneurysm claimed him in mid-life, he mounted a flamboyant campaign to reverse the devastating effects of fossil fuel combustion on the mixed mesophytic forest. With characteristic verve, he staged "the Appalachia Forest Action Project" from an old coal company house in the shadow of the A.T. Massey Performance Coal Company at Montcoal.

To get the word out, John guided a steady procession of researchers, photographers, and reporters through the forest and public establishments on Coal River. Periodicals such as the *Christian Science Monitor*, *The Charleston Gazette*, *The Amicus Journal*, and *American Forests* carried the results of these forays. He was also changing the way his neighbors were seeing the forest. "I talked to Johnny Flynn maybe a hundred times," said Dr. Jim Wills of Beckley, who grew up on Rock Creek with John Flynn, "and I didn't think his theory meant much. And then I walked the property line up to the old house, and I couldn't believe it. It looked like somebody had dropped a bomb in there. The trees were just fallen over everywhere. The big hickories where I used to squirrel hunt, all gone. The big oaks were all gone, fallen over with a big root ball sticking up. It just looked like deadfall everywhere." In 1993 John engaged me, as a representative of a national cultural institution, to listen with him to what his neighbors and relatives were noticing about their woods.

Joe Aliff, of Rock Creek, with cross section of diseased specimen

Tracking the cultural contours of forest crisis took us into nearly every hollow, coal camp, and public establishment on Coal River, from Whitesville to Arnett. John's Grand Tour began with the diseased trees and the sulfate-laden haze drawn deep into the hollows with each evening's breeze. Joe Aliff, a disabled coal miner on Rock Creek who for 20 years has tracked the effects of this "damned blue haze" on his mountain, says it comes "like a thief through the air." John would point out that this haze and its effects are intimately connected to social dramas unfolding up and down the river. He'd show people how, at the entrances to Performance, Goals, and Marfork, the United Mineworkers were staging a comeback against A.T. Massey's nonunion politics, and how the deep hollow of Shumate's Branch, home to several dozen families until the mid-1980s, is now filling with sludge—waste from the cleaning of low-sulfur coal. Several miles down the road we witnessed the struggle of a family to remain in the settlement of Packsville, enduring a rumbling procession of overloaded coal trucks 24 hours a day rather than sell their home to A.T. Massey for pennies on the dollar. A sign posted by a holdout at the mouth of Packsville highlights the interrelations of collective bargaining, place, and staying power: "UMWA is Coming Soon."

Linking all of these events behind the scenes is the Clean Air Act of 1990, which stimulated a national demand for the low-sulfur bituminous coal of the central Appalachian plateau. Permits now exist for 500 square miles of mountaintop removal and valley fill in West Virginia. Mountaintop removal, deemed the cheapest, most efficient way to recover all this low-sulfur coal, tends to rely on a mobile fleet of contractors more than on local (unionized) workers. "Do you know what the new three R's are?" Pat Canterbury of Naoma asked me in Syble's restaurant. "Remove, Remove, Reclaim."

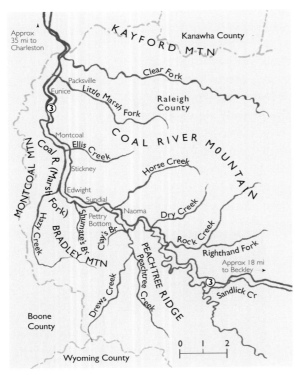

At stake in the battle over clean air is the survival of the commons—not just the commons of woods and soil—but the civic commons anchored in shared public space. We might think of commons in two senses here. One is the sense in which resources like air and water cannot be privately owned and thus are accessible to all. Protecting their quality is in the public interest. The second is the sense in which the commons comprises a realm of public discourse to which every citizen in a democracy should have access. This realm of public discourse is necessary for the cultivation of any kind of common world. Common worlds—whether national or local—are created around the physical resources in which the community has a stake—such as rivers, parks, mountains, and forests. When such physical resources become private property, the common worlds anchored in them are displaced. On Coal River, soil, water, and forest anchor a common world that is generations deep.

When we're on Coal River, Lyntha Eiler and I stay at Syble's Bed and Barn, a boarding house operated by Syble Pettry and her daughter, Crystal. Lyntha is the photographer I have been working with on this project. Most of the boarders are miners and contractors working far from their homes in places like Kentucky, Pennsylvania, and Virginia. For many who live locally, the day begins with coffee at the "Back

Porch," a restaurant with a high sociability quotient. Often the talk and teasing at the restaurant's six tables merge into a single conversation.

Like the creeks coursing their way out of the hollows, the talk in Syble's twists and turns in every direction. It pauses to unravel knots in kinship; it weaves together etymology with events; it tethers people to place; and binds flora, fauna, and topography into a seasonal round. It digresses into genealogy.

"Do you know where Jack and Buzz Williams come from?" Vernon Williams asks Joe Jarrell, a resident of Horse Creek.

"I don't know where Williams come from," Joe Jarrell replies, "But I know where their grandma come from, cause she was my grandpa's sister. Her name was Pliney. They got a hollow up there that's named for her, Pline's Hollow."

Sooner or later such talk turns to the loss of the land to industry, a history reaching back to the turn of the century when land companies bought up land and mineral rights, offering a cow or a gun for a parcel of unused ridgeland, or paying the taxes on property and trading surface rights for unobstructed access to the minerals. "That's how these big companies come in here and took this country," says Joe Jarrell, drama- tizing the historic transactions that took place by the thousands. "Okay, now 'how about a milk cow for a hundred acres of mineral?'" No one in- volved in those transactions imagined that one day machines the size of ten-story buildings would obliterate the surface entirely. Indeed, on Coal River, the slow and permanent destruction of forest species by pollutants from combusting fossil fuels is compounded by the swift and equally per- manent destruction of forest habitat to get at the coal by removing the mountaintop. "Deep mining didn't hurt the land," emphasizes Jess Duncan, a United Mineworker from Sylvester who would like to see mountaintop removal stopped and deep mining restored.

Since 1990 the coal companies have gated off accustomed routes from the valleys to the ridges, thus enclosing areas long used as com- mons for hunting, gathering, and recreation. Litanies of these lost places emerge in the talk: Marfork, Blue Pennant, Seng Creek, Bailey's Mountain, Bradley Mountain, the Head of Drew's Creek. "You can't get off the main road!" Woody Boggess once exclaimed. To understand the impact of these gates, installed ostensibly to reduce liability for acci- dents, one has to understand the historical role of the forest commons in a system of corn–woodland–pastureland farming with Cherokee and Celtic antecedents.

Rising above the farmsteads along each creek is a forested area that has historically been treated as commons, places to hunt; to gather wood, greens, and herbs; to have adventures or to be alone. The abun- dant mast of nuts and fruits such as beechnut, hickory, and walnut, and pawpaw, persimmons, and red mulberry created an ideal pastureland for cattle and hogs. Corn and beans were cultivated on flat "benches" in the forest, called "newground." Newground had to be "grubbed" of stumps, and was utilized for several years, and then "let go" in a cycle of forest fal- lowing that took several generations to complete. "My dad had new- grounds on both sides of the daggone mountain," said Kenny Pettry, one night in the Sundial Tavern, which he owns and operates with his wife Martha. "Worked us to death!"

This system of forest farming persisted well into the twentieth cen- tury, because for many decades the land subsidized the intermittent

Pawpaw on Drew's Creek

and low wages of industry. During what Mae Bongalis called "the Hoover times," reliance on wild foods minimized dependence on the company store. "Back in the bad times," Mae recalled, "I seen people go out, be snow on the ground, rake that snow and leaves off, you find little sprouts and pick it to eat. People didn't even have grease to go on the stuff they cooked. They just boiled it and ate it. And we had plenty."

Since the earliest days of settlement the woods have generated cash as well as food, shelter, and recreation. "Just about the only source of cash was from the sale of ginseng," Bob Daniels told me when I visited his saw mill on Dry Creek, named Appalachian Hardwoods. Ginseng augmented the scrip and barter economy of the coal camps. Randy Halstead, whose brokerage of nonwoody forest products infuses hundreds of thousands of dollars into the local economy, recalled "My dad was a coal miner when the union was organizing. He was involved in that, so a lot of times he was out of work. So, you send ten children to school, and working now and then, you had to make money whatever way you could. We would dig ginseng to buy our school clothes and buy our books so we could go back to school in the fall."

The historical practice of forest farming has conferred on each species an enduring identity. In conversations on Coal River, the term "tree" rarely appears; rather, trees are cited by their local names: "poplar," "lin," "buckeye," "sugar tree," "beech," "walnut," "butternut," and "mountain" or "yellow locust"—a magisterial canopy tree distinguished locally from "field" or "black" locust, a distinction that dropped out of scientific discourse in the nineteenth century. The blooms of locust, poplar, and bass are known staples in the "honey chain." Lin (bass) provided ashless, even heat for molasses-making. Yellow locust is for fence posts. Chestnut was for the rails. Hickory was the standard for sled runners, mauls, axe handles, and chairs.

However, Ben Burnside, of Rock Creek, maintains that pawpaw actually makes the best hoe handles. Though only in his sixties, Burnside is a noted local historian. His memory teems with etymology, genealogy, and the impact of history on every cove, rock, and species. "I never forget a date," says Ben. From his porch at the head of Rock Creek Hollow's Left-Hand Fork, he is discussing the vanishing nut trees with John Flynn and me: "Of course, the butternut," says Ben, "They're just about a thing of the past. Most of them are dying."

"Remember the chinquapin nuts?" John asks him.

"They're gone too, ain't they?" Ben observes.

Not entirely, according to Mae Bongalis. "Chinquapins is about all died out, but there's one tree growing up Sandlick," she tells us later. "I seen this little branch a-hanging by the door of that little market right by the road. And the guy that owns that place, he's a good friend, and I said, 'Beano, where did you get them chinquapins?' He said, 'You know, Mae, nobody knows what they are, how did you know?' I says, 'I picked many a one of them.'" The chinquapin, a shrubby chestnut species, is sensitive to the toxic mix of acid rain, ozone, and excess nitrogen generated by distant combustion of fossil fuels. "That damned blue haze," as Joe Aliff describes it.

Behind such comments as Mae Bongalis' about the disappearing chinquapins is the concept of the seasonal round, a practice that ties the forest to community life and synchronizes gardening, hunting, gathering, and the marketplace. "For each season there is something to do," explained David Bailey of Stickney. "If you were growing up in this neck of the woods, in the spring, when the weeds grow up and the trees bud out, you get mushrooms. You get greens. That's in the spring. Then it gets a little warmer, you go fishing. On up through about July, that's about the beginning of summer. Blackberries. You pick raspberries. Then on up into about August, there's apples. Then, September, October, there's hickory nuts, there's beech nuts. There's walnuts, on up to about December, and that's about all until spring rolls around." The seasonal round is a primary cultural resource—which would be greatly diminished by the loss of the forest to air pollution.

The seasonal round's incorporation into community life is everywhere in evidence: in the six-pronged ginseng "trophy" mounted on the wall behind the bar in the Sundial Tavern; in the old Wills newground that Ivan Jarrell plants in winter with browse for deer; and in the hillside that Woody Boggess has smothered in ramps transplanted from Hazy when the gates were about to go up. The seasonal round is embodied in food cellars stocked with jars of garden produce, wild greens, berries, and nuts; in Randy Sprouse's venison jerky, Glenna Bailey's strawberry cookies, Nancy Bailey's beechnut persimmon cake, and Mae Bongalis' black walnut pumpkin roll.

Ramps and ginseng, two of the most culturally important non-woody species, do best in the rich soils of the coves. Ramps, wild cousins of leeks and the first of the wild foods to appear in the spring,

Glenna Bailey, of Stickney, paring potatoes for "deer soup"

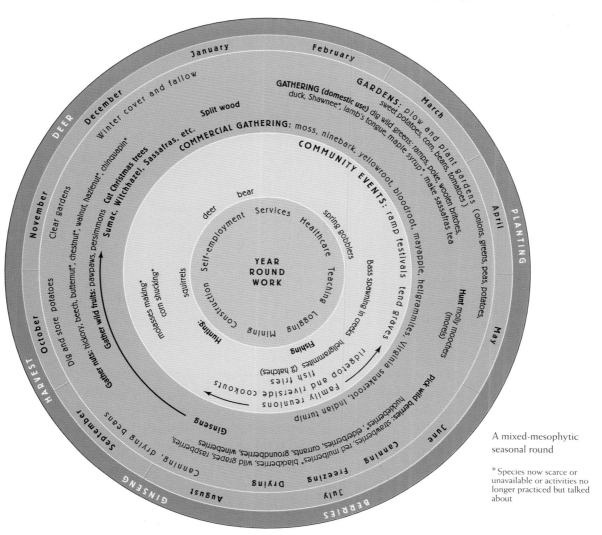

A mixed-mesophytic seasonal round

* Species now scarce or unavailable or activities no longer practiced but talked about

are featured at spring feasts throughout the southern mountains, together with boisterous jokes about the odor ramps bestow on their loyal consumers. The annual ramp supper at Drew's Creek is approaching its fiftieth year. "There's a thousand and one different ways to eat them," one patron told me when I attended. "I like mine pickled."

On Coal River, "seng hoes" are standard household implements, remodelled by their users from old garden hoes, fire pokers, and automobile springs. "They used to take old mine picks when they'd wear out and cut them off at the blacksmith shop," Mae Bongalis told me. "They make a good one."

Woody Boggess, in the ramp patch he planted behind his home in Pettry Bottom

Ginseng is both noun and verb. "There's an art to ginsenging now," said Ed Cantley when John Flynn and I visited him at the head of Rock Creek, where he raises Christmas trees and ornamental birds. "Once you learn it you never forget it." Ernie Scarbro, Ben Burnside's neighbor, looks for ginseng around sugar maples, black gum, and hickory. "Squirrels are in the hickories and the berries get ripe, and they eat them. So it makes for a lot of ginseng around the hickories."

Taking their cue from the squirrels, diggers propagate the plant—sowing the seeds where ginseng is known to grow, sometimes replanting the stalk with a piece of the rhizome (called the "curl") attached. "I'll come back some year and get another root off of that," said Joe Williams of Leevale as he carefully packed rich dirt around a replanted stalk of seng in Tom's Hollow.

In conversations about tree death on Coal River, the fate of the commons looms large. "I'll tell you what's dying here," says David Stover, naturalist at the Twin Falls State Park in Mullens, West Virginia, "the concept that the forest itself was open—that the land was like air or water. Who could own it?"

Anchored in the physical spaces of the commons is a common world that is one of the great cultural works on Coal River. Over generations of social construction in story and in practice, places on this commons have accrued a dense, historical residue. Every wrinkle rippling the mountains has been named for people, flora, fauna, practices, and events both singular and recurrent: "Each hollow has a name," said Dennis Dickens, an octogenarian we spoke with on Peachtree Creek. Onto a scrap of drywall, Ben Burnside fixed the names of the hollows along Rock Creek so they wouldn't be forgotten. The names index and weave together elements of corn–woodland–pastureland farming and community life: Calf Hollow, Bee Comb Hollow, Big Lick Hollow, School House Hollow, Pawpaw Hollow, Mill Hollow, Stockingleg Hollow, Coon Hollow, Canterbury Hollow, Sugar Camp Hollow, and Hollow Field. "Somebody must have had a newground in there," Burnside told us. Sandstone camping rocks protruding from ridges are thresholds to stories of other ancestors—Jake Rock, John Rock, Turkey Rock, Crane Rock, Charlie Rock, and the Marrying Rock, where couples used to await the blessing of the circuit rider. "Every big rock is named," said Pat Canterbury, speaking to the Lucy Braun Association in Mt. Vernon, Kentucky.

More than 50 years ago, miners camping while hunting and digging ginseng inscribed their initials on the John Rock with carbide lamps. Charred flat rocks and rocks pocked with cone-shaped mortars, which Mae Bongalis' grandmother showed her as they gathered herbs, marked the places where her Indian ancestors ground corn and baked flat bread. The Coal River is segmented into dozens of holes for fishing, swimming, and baptisms that also anchor the common world: Turn Hole, the Ed Jarrell Hole, the Sawmill Hole, Snake Den Hole, and the Garden Hole, where "that big bass broke Cuby Wiley's fifty-pound line."

But it isn't only the depth of the past, indexed in dozens and dozens of such sites, that gives the commons its value. It is the historical openness of the commons, where almost anything can happen. In the social imagination, conjured through stories of plying the commons, the commons becomes a proving ground on which attributes of courage, loyalty, belonging, stamina, wit, foolishness, honesty, judgment, and luck are continuously displayed and evaluated.

American ginseng

"Tell me a story," says John Flynn to Danny Williams, up on Clay's Branch.

"What do you want to hear?" Danny asks him. "A lie?"

"I want to hear a good Danny Williams story. A fairly clean story," John teases.

"I'll tell you one," says Danny. "Me and Gregory and—"

"Now he's going to tell a lie," protests Gregory, Danny's brother.

Danny ignores him. "—and that son of mine were out ginsenging in the mountains, and Gregory got hurt, he got his hand cut off and they sewed it back."

"He's going to tell a lie," insists Gregory.

"And we were sitting there resting. And we looked, and here come a man walking around the side of the hill. And it was Jesus, and he walked up to us, and he looked at DJ, he said, 'DJ, do you believe?'

"DJ said, 'Well, Lord, sometimes I do, sometimes I don't, and sometimes I just don't know.'

"Jesus said, 'Is there anything that bothers you?'

"DJ said, 'Yes, my arm bothers me a lot.'

"The Lord reached down, he touched his arm, and he said, 'Well, you're healed.' And DJ twisted that arm around, up and down, he said, 'That arm ain't never felt that good.'

"Jesus looked over at me, and he said, 'Do you believe?' I said, 'Well, I'm like DJ. Sometimes I do, sometimes I don't, and sometimes I just don't know.'

"He said, 'Well, you got anything that bothers you?'

"I said, 'My legs bother me. They hurt all the time.' He reached over and he touched my legs, and he said, 'They're healed.' They quit hurting.

"Then Jesus looked at Gregory, and said, 'Gregory, do you believe?'

"Gregory said, 'Hold it right there, Lord. Don't come no closer.' He said, 'I'm on compensation.' "

"Told you he was going to tell a big one, now didn't I?" declares Gregory.

Reflecting later on Danny's "lie" and the conversation in which it was set, I saw in it a parable of the national system that supports forest deterioration, our topic that afternoon. America, acting in bad faith, perpetuates a system that makes inflicting and sustaining injury—to people and environment—more profitable than healing. Danny's story about a mythic encounter while ginsenging on the commons illuminates what urbanist Marshall Berman has called "the ethical, moral, and social abyss" at the heart of a system that inflicts injury with one hand while providing therapy with the other.

Our national system of classifying land and resources shatters the coherence of local landscapes long before bulldozers lay blades to them. The sludge impounded at Shumate's Branch provides a case in point. To find out how it was possible to transform Shumate's Branch, a hollow rich in vegetable gardens, ramps, ginseng, history, and community life, into a "slurry pond," one has to consult the records of many agencies—the U.S. Environmental Protection Agency, the state Division of Environmental Protection, U.S. Fish and Wildlife, the state Division of Culture and History, the Soil Conservation Service—all arrayed around it like medical specialists at an autopsy. Of special interest are three claims made by the Peabody Coal Company regarding the environmental and cultural impact of the proposed Shumate Creek Refuse Disposal Area. The company reported that it found (1) no prime farmland or history of growing crops, even though former residents recall vegetable gardens from the head of the hollow to its

Black slurry (wet refuse from the cleaning of coal) fills the hollow of Shumate's Branch

mouth; (2) no historic resources (after moving a family cemetery 10 miles down the road); and (3) no endangered species, even though today former residents talk about the wealth of ginseng that grew there.

The commons of the soil, particularly rich soil for cultivating crops, is protected by the Surface Mining Control and Reclamation Act of 1977, which requires that companies "rebuild the horizons" if they disturb prime farmland. While land with a deep history of subsistence gardening qualifies as prime farmland, the Soil Conservation Service has classified less than half of 1 percent of West Virginia soil as prime farmland. "There's no prime farmland in Raleigh County," said Charlie Sturry, of the state's Division of Environmental Protection. Because the standards for prime farmland were developed in the Midwest, anything smaller than an acre is not registered on Soil Conservation Service maps, which form the basis for environmental impact assessments.

In other words, although they probably contain more organic matter and humus than soils found on the alluvial plains, the flat "benches" riddling the mountains are considered too small to take note of. "My grandma used to send us into the coves with sacks to get dirt for the garden each spring," recalled Pat Canterbury. "It was so rich you didn't need a shovel. Just scoop it up with your hands."

Such testimonials to the richness of the cove soils contradict the national stereotype of poor, farmed-out mountain hills. Codified in Soil Conservation Service maps, this stereotype streamlines industry's access to coal. "Breaking New Ground," the title of the A.T. Massey Coal Company's public relations video, is thus ironically apt. The film celebrates the vision of E. Morgan Massey on his retirement. Massey's vision, according to the video, led him to influence clean air legislation, to stake out a sizeable share of the low-sulfur coal in West Virginia and Kentucky, and to establish a "union-free" climate for running coal. This vision, stunningly Faustian in character and in scope, is radically transforming the forests of the central Appalachian plateau.

The decisions that shape the landscape on Coal River are made in offices scattered around the country—in offices of the Rowland Land Company in Charleston and Pittsburgh, for instance; in Richmond, Virginia, where the A.T. Massey Coal Company is headquartered; and in San Francisco, where its parent company, the multinational Fluor Corporation is based. The devastated landscapes and dying forests they are producing embody what Marshall Berman, in his book *All that is Solid Melts into Air*, terms "Faustian creativity."

There can be no finer example of Faustian creativity than mountaintop removal. Devotees of the method emphasize the creative aspects of reclamation and the greater good achieved for society as a whole. "As a result of mining in the mountaintop method," explained Roger Hall, assistant director of the state's Division of Environmental Protection, "you've actually developed a lot of usable land which has some future potential for industrial and commercial use." This potential is laid out in *Greenlands*, the industry's glossy public relations magazine. One reclaimed site is a hay field. Another is a state-of-the-art golf course. Another has garnered an award from Ducks Unlimited for wetlands reconstruction. The Princess Beverly Coal Company recently won the state's Mountaineer Guardian Award for reclamation plantings on this plateau that included Siberian crabapple, deer tongue, silky dogwood, and Chinese chestnut—all non-native species.

The net result is a geometric patchwork interspersed with forested hills, which Lyntha Eiler and I toured by helicopter in the company of Benny Campbell, a mining inspector for the state's Department of Environmental Protection. From the air we identify the species by their fall colors: the rich yellows of hickory, the bright red of sourwood, the blazing orange of maples. Emerging out of the forested hills is a Faustian pastiche, which looks from the air as though it were wrought with ease by giant cookie cutters and rolling pins. "That's a big valley fill behind us," says Campbell. "And down there is a small mom and pop operation." All around us on the horizon we could pick out the rocky ribbons of exposed highwall, the emerald green laminated beneath the green veneer of lespedeza (commonly known as "saw grass"), the electric yellows and greens of catchment basins, the bright black ooze of slurry ponds, the chevrons of rock-lined drainage systems, and the switchback roads crisscrossing the stepped impoundments holding the valley fill. A Biblical text popped into my mind: "Let the valleys be raised and the mountains laid low."

The piéce de rèsistance here is the dragline, a technological wonder ten stories high, equipped with a 53-cubic-yard scoop. One of these machines is nicknamed "Big John." "You gotta see it," says Campbell. "It's a big machine that removes rock and spoil and overburden so that the machinery can get into the coal seam itself and load the coal out." We viewed the dragline in operation on the Cabin Creek plateau, briskly dismantling mountains that were almost immediately being reassembled into a patchwork of precision-engineered curves and angles.

I wondered how much ginseng gets bulldozed. Under the Convention on International Trade in Endangered Species (CITES), the law provides for stiff fines and possible incarceration of anyone caught with green ginseng in their possession out of season. Does this law criminalize the offseason removal of ginseng by the ton, in a region that supplies more than half of the nation's annual wild export? "They're not harvesting it," explained Bob Whipkey, who monitors the harvest and export of ginseng for the state's Division of Forestry. "They're destroying it, but the law only regulates the harvest."

Conversing with me in the Rowland Land Company's plush quarters in Charleston, David Pollitt and his uncle Howard emphasize their contributions to community life through jobs the company has enabled over the past century, the many leases it provides very cheaply, and its donation of buildings for schools and land for a housing development for miners. "People complain about absentee landowners," said Howard Pollitt with unintended irony, "But without absentee landowners, there wouldn't even be a West Virginia." The land companies belong to an association, the National Council of Coal Lessors, which employs a full-time lobbyist to protect its members against the regulation of fossil fuels that are threatening the forest both through localized destruction and the long-range transport of air pollution.

"And I weathered the storm" says the epitaph on the tombstone of Donnie Wills, just across the road from where John Flynn is buried. On Coal River, the dead are helping to defend the living. Along the 20-mile stretch between Glen Daniel and Whitesville there are hundreds of known cemeteries, and many more whose locations have been forgotten, that have subsided into brush and obscurity. Stories of disturbing the dead are related with a kind of horror: the coffin that fell into a break where miners were working, the black cemetery near Birchton Curve that a coal company bulldozed into a ditch, the possibility that bodies were not really moved when the Peabody Company relocated the community cemetery on Shumate's Branch.

Cemeteries are sacred enough that the Surface Mining Control and Reclamation Act bans mining within 300 feet of them. People with family buried behind the company gates are permitted to visit the cemeteries, which form an archipelago of tiny preserves in a shifting Faustian sea. Once a year, on Memorial Day, when the cemeteries are alive with descendants cleaning and decorating graves, the gates at the Sundial prep plant are left open.

On that day the descendants of Belle Wilson drive through the open gate to tend their ancestral cemetery at Shumate's Branch. They converge from Washington, D.C., northern New Jersey, Ohio, and elsewhere to hold their annual reunion and to honor loved ones buried on "Graveyard Hill."

Many who tend the graves were dispersed when the Armco Corporation closed the mines at Edwight in the 1950s. People scattered north and south, to Ohio, New Jersey, and back to Alabama. Belle Wilson took the lumber from the Church of God and built a new home 60 miles away in Switzer, in Logan County. Beyond honoring their loved ones, one reason the family returns year after year is to ensure the survival of the cemetery.

Tending cemeteries thus becomes a way of maintaining a place on a precarious landscape, of staving off cultural disappearance. Tending cemeteries is a way of ensuring the survival of public space, which is essential to the survival of the civic commons. "If the world is to contain a public space," wrote the noted political scientist Hannah Arendt, "it cannot be erected for one generation and planned for the living only; it must transcend the life-span of mortal men."

There are many stories of cultural survival on Coal River. I see this survival as the continual staging of reappearance, of counteracting industry's message that nothing really happens here. "Massey Coal came in and said, 'You don't exist,'" John Flynn once told me. On the application for the Shumate Creek Refuse Disposal Area, there is no indication that it was ever settled and farmed. The reclamation plan, for "forest and wildlife habitat," includes plantings of gray dogwood, European black alder, autumn olive, and Japanese bayberry—nitrogen-fixing species that may set the stage for the eventual return of native hardwoods. Then again, they may not. The impact of mountaintop removal on the mixed mesophytic system has yet to be addressed, though it should be a matter for public debate.

As a social and cultural institution with roots in antiquity, the commons predates the idea of private property. The ongoing process of converting commons into "resources" began in England during the Enlightenment. There the social and environmental effects of destroying the commons included irreversible deforestation, degradation of soils and water, homelessness, and the emergence of the world's first industrial working class.

Missing in the national environmental policy debate is any recognition of the geographic commons and its critical role in community life. As the object that both unites and separates those gathered around it, the commons sustains the public sphere. Violation of the geographic commons annuls the civic commons. "They're taking our dignity by destroying our forest," says Vernon Williams of Peachtree Creek. Neglecting the value of the commons and covering up the human costs, we, like Faust, continue to forge our pact with Mephistopheles.

Call to Action

So far this book has dealt with the effects of pollution on the forests of the Appalachian Mountains, with the ecological and cultural implications of such pollution, and with transgressions such as strip mining and clearcutting of the forests.

Now we will take up the industrial *origins* of air and water pollution, beginning with a pair of photographs—one taken during the nighttime and one at sunrise—of a paper mill that is a kind of round-the-clock, triple-threat polluter. This factory produces not only air pollution, but water pollution and clearcuts, too, for its raw materials are trees reduced to a fibrous slurry for the manufacture of envelopes. In the process, in 1994 Champion's Canton mill pumped 4.6 million pounds of toxins into the atmosphere (the most recent data available at the time of writing), including 3.1 million pounds of methanol, a greenhouse gas and ozone precursor, and 810,000 pounds of stack gasses of the kind that contribute to acid rain. As for water pollution, between 1990 and 1994 the Champion plant discharged 1.33 million pounds of toxic chemicals into the Pigeon River.

The foregoing air pollution data were drawn from the "TRI," the Environmental Protection Agency's *Toxic Release Inventory*. Because of the TRI, established by law in 1985 (albeit narrowly; the House vote was 212 to 211), some 25,000 plants and factories are now forced to report their releases of designated air pollutants (300 are listed at present) on an annual basis. Unlike most governmentally collected statistics (often by agencies that would just as soon not have them publicized), the TRI must be made available on computer disk and via the Internet, as well as in hard copy, so that anyone who is plugged in to the land of racing electrons can have access to the numbers and crunch them in various ways. The data are posted annually, although there is a 2-year lag.

The commercial users of the inventory include insurance companies, stockbrokers, and economic development officials, aside from environmental regulators. While industry fudged statistics as a matter

Nighttime view of Champion International Corporation's paper mill, Canton, North Carolina

of course before the TRI became law (actual toxic-chemical releases turned out to be six times what the Chemical Manufacturers Association asserted before TRI), experts now believe industry figures are relatively accurate, since if corporations were caught in outright lying they might be subject to lawsuits by those with deep enough pockets to litigate them successfully.

However, the most powerful customer of the TRI, at least potentially, is the environmental activist who can analyze the data locally and bring pressure to bear on the worst offenders, and who can lobby policy makers and the EPA to improve the reporting, which is still spotty for some industries. Those proficient on the World Wide Web can access the inventory data directly (http://www.epa.gov/opptintr/tri) or through RTK.NET, an online distributor of right-to-know data (http://www.rtk.net). Hard copy for the TRI can be ordered from the EPA directly, at (800) 535-0202.

In fact, photographer Jenny Hager used the TRI to determine which industrial plants to photograph—always from vantage points that were near, though not on, company property. All but a few of her pictures are of facilities among the TRI's top 50 polluters.

Sunrise at the Champion paper mill in Canton

Welcome to the Greenhouse

Facing page, Ashland Oil Company refinery, West Elizabeth, Pennsylvania

An oil refinery strikes twice. First, the pollution the refinery itself produces is carried aloft on prevailing winds to descend on the forests of the Appalachians in the form of acid deposition, excess nitrogen, and tropospheric ozone. And then, in a more general way, ecologically disastrous global warming results from the burning of the refinery's product by factories, automobiles, houses, and office buildings.

Thanks to air pollution laws, emissions from refineries and other industrial plants have been controlled, especially sulfur dioxide (as have oxides of nitrogen, though not enough to greatly relieve Appalachian forests). But the carbon dioxide (CO_2) cannot be reduced, except by reducing the amount of fuel burned. Therefore, as long as the United States and the world remain dependent on petroleum and other fossil fuels, the carbon will continue to be converted to CO_2, producing an artificial climate change that ecosystems, including the forest ecosystems of the Appalachians, simply cannot keep up with.

In the consensus view of 2,500 scientists assembled by the United Nations, global temperatures will increase by 1.8 to 6.3 degrees Fahrenheit over the next 100 years. Forest ecosystems can adapt to warming, but they cannot pick up and move, like people; they migrate slowly, species by species. They cannot outrun a temperature rise over the next 100 years, courtesy of fossil fuels, that would ordinarily take Mother Nature 10,000 years to equal. Suddenly confronted by a hostile environment, the forests inevitably weaken—indeed already have done so—and the trees die.

United Refining Company plant operating at night, Warren, Pennsylvania

Stacking the Deck

In the 1960s the federal government, concerned about the local effects of air pollution from power-generating plants and other industrial facilities, came up with their answer to the problem. "The solution to pollution is dilution," they said. If stack gasses, especially if reduced through electrostatic "scrubbing" devices, were pumped into the high-altitude atmosphere, they would be dispersed over such a wide area that their impact would be diminished to practically zero. Accordingly, the regular stacks were taken down and new ones built, sometimes thousands of feet high.

In spite of the view held by many environmentalists that the proposition was counter-intuitive, based on the simple premise that what goes up must come down, the industrial pollution experts of the day dismissed these concerns and plunged ahead with stack-building. The result was that local, or "ambient," pollution was greatly reduced in the areas where the tall stacks were located. The only trouble was the pollution *did* come down. It came down, not as the same material sent up the stacks, but as acid precipitation visited on forests at a great distance, the Appalachian forests particularly.

Facing page and below, the Gavin electrical power plant, Cheshire County, Ohio

Left, American Electric Power, Kammer plant, West Virginia

Odorless, Colorless, Deadly

Most carbon monoxide (CO), an extremely poisonous invisible and odor-free gas, is generated by automobile engines as a waste product from incomplete combustion. In 1994 highway vehicles produced 62 percent of total national CO emissions. Even though vehicles are to blame for most of it, large quantities of the gas are still discharged by industrial plants and factories. Among manufacturing industries, steel mills are the largest source of carbon monoxide.

The coke ovens of the LTV mill "going off" (in the vernacular phrase) and the midmorning stack emissions of the USX mills, as shown on these pages and the pages following, amply demonstrate why such mills

remain a concern for public health as well as ecological reasons. The USX-Edgar Thomson Works is ranked number one in the United States among facilities emitting carbon monoxide. LTV, which is slated to be closed, is ranked 22nd.

Even though it ordinarily requires confined spaces to be fatal, the dangers of CO are still frightening: air containing one-tenth of 1 percent carbon monoxide, which takes the place of oxygen in the blood, can bring death. Moreover, CO reacts photo-chemically to produce compounds that in turn react with nitrogen oxide, causing tropospheric ozone levels to rise, which limits photosynthesis in trees, just as CO limits oxygen in humans.

Left, the LTV Steel Company plant, Pittsburgh, Pennsylvania

Top, the USX-Edgar Thompson steel mill, Pittsburgh, Pennsylvania

Below, the USX-Clairton Works steel mill, coke oven emissions, Pittsburgh, Pennsylvania

Coke oven emissions at the USX-Clairton Works steel mill on the Monongahela River, Pittsburgh, Pennsylvania—the largest coke oven in the United States

Before the Dawn

Photographer Jenny Hager often selected her factory photo sites during the pre-dawn darkness, to give her time to find the best location (near, but not on company property) for her tripod and then get a good sunrise shot. With the sun low, the sharp angles of the industrial facilities would be cast into vivid relief and the sense of perspective enhanced. While going about her business of setting up, she noticed that quite often the emissions would stop at sunrise, particularly at chemical plants. Her inquiries to government officials about whether this was common practice yielded no clear answers.

She did find that the EPA is currently readying a system to determine emissions levels at all times, not just in the daylight, with a laser device that may help to answer the question of amounts, since not all stacks have built-in emission monitors. Meanwhile, concerned citizens, after identifying major polluters from EPA's *Toxic Release Inventory* described in the introduction to this chapter, could take up emissions patrols themselves.

Quite possibly there are good reasons for shutting down the stacks at dawn. Or perhaps Jenny's experience was simply a series of coincidences. Whatever the case, these predawn photographs, taken with 4-minute exposures, show that something is actually going on in these plants, that something is actually coming out of those stacks.

Facing page, Columbian Chemicals plant, near Woodland, West Virginia

Right, BASF/Lenzing Fiber Corporation plant, Lowland, Tennessee

Below, Amoco Chemicals Company, Decatur, Alabama

Of Human Health and Ecosystems

For the most part, the U.S. government, the news media, and environmental organizations deal with air pollution in terms of human health. Asthma, lung cancer, emphysema, and associated pulmonary problems are on the rise. Particulate matter and "VOCs"—volatile organic chemicals—are implicated in the general increase in cancer, cardiovascular disease, and premature death. Incinerators, such as those shown on these pages, can be particularly menacing, which is why citizens' organizations fight so passionately against them.

But it is also true and no less significant that many of these same pollutants are causing death and disease in our most elementary life-support systems, including the forest ecosystems of the Appalachian Mountains. In a sense, these systems are even more vulnerable than we are, and their collapse over the long term will have appalling consequences. Our forests are essential for the very air we breathe and the species they contain are the building blocks of life on earth. Indeed, forest health and human health are not only linked, but consequential. The latter depends utterly on the former.

Top, Tennessee Eastman Company incinerator, Kingsport, Tennessee

Left, Carolina Power and Light electrical generating plant, near Skyland, North Carolina

The Deadly Machine

They are produced by the tens of millions every year. The American way of life is no longer frontier oriented, but automobile oriented. Cities are organized around them. Our ability to work is organized around them. Our leisure time and recreation are organized around them. Indeed, without its automotive base, our economy would collapse.

And yet it is the automobile and its use that, more than any other constituent of the political economy of industrialized nations, threatens the continuation of life on earth in any form that most humans would consider acceptable. "No more than one or a few decades remain," warned a majority of the world's scientific Nobel laureates in 1993, "before the chance to avert the threat we now confront will be lost and the prospects for humanity immeasurably diminished."

Chief among the threats that can diminish the prospects for humanity is the tropospheric ozone (smog) created by automobiles, which threatens ecosystems at vast distances from cities and interstates.

Traffic on Key Bridge, Washington, D.C.

Furthermore, the protective stratospheric ozone shield is thinned by chlorofluorocarbons leaking from radiators long after derelict cars have been sent to their graveyards. Meanwhile, by increasing temperatures in the troposphere, global warming (to which automobiles contribute massively) decreases them in the stratosphere. Moreover, because the O_3 molecule is more easily broken down in extreme cold, some scientists fear that the decreased temperatures may lead to a self-perpetuating thinning of the ozone shield, despite efforts to reduce CFC production.

Left and below, cars produce a variety of pollutants—gasses, liquids, and solids

Bottom, traffic in the Georgetown area, Washington, D.C.

Heat Island

warmer than in countryside areas surrounding cities.

As the thermometer rises, the air conditioners are turned on. This not only produces heat from the electric motors that drive the compressors but also transfers heat from the inside of buildings to the outside, where it is already roasting because of the heat gain from sun on asphalt paving, bricks, and other dense materials. By nighttime so much heat has been

Here is a perfect example of a disastrous feedback loop created by cheap fossil fuel energy. It is what's called the urban "heat island" effect, where temperatures are between 9 and 12 degrees (Fahrenheit)

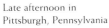
Late afternoon in Pittsburgh, Pennsylvania

absorbed by these materials that the temperature level remains high, requiring that air conditioners be run even when ambient conditions would seem not to require it.

Studies have shown that about 30 percent of the air pollution generated by cities is due to the heat-island effect, a problem with widespread consequences. As the heat island gets hotter and hotter (and larger and larger in the case of growing cities), more and more CO_2-generating fossil fuel energy is required to cool it. This produces more and more global warming and the increasing breakdown of forest ecosystems in a spiral whose end point is fearful to contemplate.

Air conditioners, Washington, D.C.

The Palmerton Legacy

Emily, photographer Jenny Hager's daughter, is shown in this moonscape with dead trees just 50 yards west of the Appalachian Trail, which here traverses Blue Mountain. Behind Emily, just over the rise, is a zinc factory (shown in the smaller picture), part of which is now idle and part of which still operates. Zinc smelting, which caused all this damage, began in 1898 and was suspended in 1980. The EPA calls the general area the "Palmerton Zinc Pile." The pile covers about 2,000 acres, encompassing Blue Mountain, which was once heavily forested but whose soils have been lifeless for decades. According to the EPA, the ambient air is contaminated with heavy

Emily, age 6, explores an area just off the Appalachian Trail near Palmerton, Pennsylvania

metals (lead, cadmium, and zinc), as is the water. They report that children in Palmerton have elevated levels of cadmium and lead in their hair and blood. So do horse and cattle, which have shown "substantiated cases" of illness and fatigue.

There are other places like this in the Appalachians, most notably at Ducktown, Tennessee, where nineteenth- and early twentieth-century copper smelting took place, desertifying a 56-square-mile area

that in some places has never recovered.

These are lessons from the past. The devastations took place under conditions that no longer exist. Even so, a visit to Palmerton, or Ducktown, or any place in the Appalachians where greed and heedlessness have destroyed the forest, can be vividly instructive concerning the effects of industrial pollution on our irreplaceable ecosystems.

Palmerton zinc factory, Palmerton, Pennsylvania

If the Truth Be Told

Is the photograph on this page a picture of the future? Or will the children soon arrive, and somehow the factory in the background magically disappear and the woodlands return? The fact is, we really do have a choice.

The problem is despair. Environmental despair wears two faces today. The first says "nothing can be done." That is what politicians, industrialists, and even some environmentalists believe. So entrenched are they in seeing the future in a certain way, that they cannot conceive of a truly better world, only one with more "growth." Growth for the sake of growth, as Edward Abbey pointed out, is the etiology of the cancer cell.

The second face of despair says "nothing is the matter." And this, even more than the first, is the idea we must resist. There are those—*the confusionists*, as some call them—who knowingly manipulate statistics to conceal the truth about such issues as global warming, the ozone hole, and acid rain. They say the Appalachian forests are healthy, have never been better, no need to worry. People listen of course because they wish to believe it, to be relieved of anxiety.

Such an avoidance of reality is pathological and can infect large numbers of people unless it is resolutely countered with scientific fact, logical analysis, and full public discussion. Only if the truth be told can any real hope for the future emerge, for hope without truth is not hope at all but merely propaganda.

In Phil Shabecoff's essay, which follows, you will read about these issues as they unfolded in the decade of the 1980s and are unfolding even now for the forests of the Appalachians. So please read on, but then, as Phil urges, *act*!

A playground in Kingsport, Tennessee, with the Willamette pulp and paper mill in the background

After Decades of Deception, a Time to Act

by Philip Shabecoff

Exhaustion is apparent on every hand—exhaustion of soil, exhaustion of men, exhaustion of hopes. Weariness and lethargy have settled closer everywhere.... The nation—engulfed in its money-making and international politics—has paid no noticeable heed to its darkest area.

It is time—well past time—to pay heed.

The words above were written more than 30 years ago by Harry M. Caudill in his landmark book, *Night Comes to the Cumberlands*, to describe the human and ecological debility that was then settling over the depressed, ravished, and neglected highlands of Appalachia. The timber companies had torn the trees from the hillsides, letting the soil wash from the steep slopes into the once clear streams. The coal mines bore into the hills and deep into the earth, piling huge mounds of slag that leached their acids into the region's soil and waters. The hills themselves were sliced to the floors of the narrow valleys by the huge earth-moving machines of the strip mines. When the seams were exhausted or the market for coal was slumping, the mines simply closed, leaving behind a desolate landscape, jobless miners with blackened lungs, demoralized communities, and no foundation for an economy to replace mining, lumbering, or the traditional small-scale farming that had preceded them.

And yet, as one of the region's civic groups has pointed out, "Appalachia is a land of contradictions: rich yet poor, exploited yet underdeveloped, scarred yet beautiful." Despite the years of timbering and mining, the region remains heavily forested, a land lovely with dogwood and redbud, oak and hickory, beech, tulip poplar and basswood and, in its southern end, with deep, fragrant pine woods.

On an autumn morning nearly two decades ago, while gathering material for an article on the Appalachian Trail, I took a walk with some companions along a portion of the trail near Harpers Ferry, West Virginia, a few hour's drive from Washington, D.C. At the top of a high ridge, we paused at a break in the forest to look out over a vista stunning in its beauty. The bowl-shaped valley and the hills beyond were an unbroken mass of trees whose orange and russet and golden leaves

Pennsylvania Power's
Bruce Mansfield Plant,
Beaver, Pennsylvania

seemed to capture and enhance the bright October sunshine. A U.S. Forest Service biologist who accompanied our party quipped that "Every one of those leaves was hand painted. It was hard work." But no human hands could have created that resplendent panorama.

Now, less than a generation later, many of those trees are sick or dying. Throughout much of the region, air pollution is scarring and thinning the forests. Even the solace of beauty is being denied people in many hard pressed areas of Appalachia. They are also losing the wood, nuts, fruit, shade, wildlife, watershed protection, oxygen, and tranquillity that the forest provides them.

Despite the wide and mounting body of scientific evidence. . . the long history of neglect of Appalachia's sorrows continues.

Once again, the land and people of the nation's "darkest area" have fallen victim to the careless indifference of big, powerful, and distant corporations and to the ineptitude of the government response which, corrupted as usual by the influence of vested interests, is too little, too late. Once again, Appalachia is paying a heavy price for economic benefits in which it does not fully share.

While there are still skeptics within the scientific community, the weight of evidence has long demonstrated that air pollution from power plants, smelters, factories, and automobiles is a major threat to the forests in the eastern part of the United States. For Appalachia, of course, the great irony is that much of that pollution comes from the coal that was taken at such high costs from its own soil and shipped as a cheap fuel to distant electric-generating plants. The gases from the burning coal, ejected through the tall stacks of the power plants, are carried from the Midwest by the eastward-blowing winds to return to the hills and valleys of Appalachia as oxides of sulfur and nitrogen that settle on the land and its trees as acid rain, or fog, or snow, or dry particles. Other pollutants, such as volatile organic chemicals, mingle with the acid to form a noxious stew that settles over the trees, penetrates

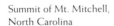

Summit of Mt. Mitchell, North Carolina

into the leaves and needles, and seeps into the ground, altering the soil and depleting the nutrients and microorganisms that permit the trees to be nourished, to grow and remain healthy.

Despite the wide and mounting body of scientific evidence, despite the increasingly visible evidence of dead and dying trees, and despite the growing public outcry, the long history of neglect of Appalachia's sorrows continues.

Acid rain is not a new discovery. In 1873, more than a century ago, a British chemist named Robert Angus Smith established a link between the sulfuric acid in the black coal smoke that belched continuously from the stacks of heavily industrialized Manchester and the acid rain that regularly fell on the city and its vicinity. By the 1940s European scientists had confirmed that oxides of sulfur and nitrogen released by the combustion of fossil fuels such as coal and oil are converted in the atmosphere to sulfates and nitrates which, combined with moisture in the atmosphere, return to earth as acid precipitation.

But the broad, long-term effects of pollution such as acid rain on ecological systems remained little understood or ignored in the rush to industrialize in Europe and North America. Whatever threat air pollution might present to the environment or public health was thought to be of little or no consequence except in the immediate area of the source of pollution. Slowly, however, the insidious effects of acid rain and other air pollution on the landscape and people became apparent, as did the fact that pollution could be carried long distances from the tall stacks used to disperse it and wreak its damage many hundreds of miles from its source. By the early 1970s, scientists and political leaders in Sweden and Norway were becoming increasingly alarmed over the impact of air pollution, particularly acid rain drifting over from Central Europe and Britain, acidifying their lakes and damaging the trees and crops. It was this Scandinavian alarm signal, in fact, that led the United Nations to convene the UN Conference on Human Development in Stockholm in 1972.

When the U.S. Congress finally passed the landmark Clean Air Act of 1970, it set ambient air quality standards limiting the amount of pollution that a factory, power plant, smelter, motor vehicles, and other sources were permitted to send into the surrounding air. This slowly began to reduce the grosser forms of air pollution such as the thick black particles that had darkened the sky over industrial areas and major cities. Those standards, however, protected only the airsheds surrounding the polluting facilities. Coal-fired power plants and other polluting industries sought to meet the standards chiefly by building taller smokestacks that sent the emissions of sulfur, nitrogen, and solid particles high into the atmosphere, where they were carried by prevailing winds away from the surrounding airshed, often to be deposited many hundreds of miles away. Industry long resisted more expensive solutions, such as installing scrubbers to remove the pollution before it emerged from the stacks, technology to clean coal, or simply buying more expensive low-sulfur coal. Public utilities argued that the costs to electricity consumers and the impact on local industry would outweigh the

Two decades after the passage of the 1970 law, most of the nation's major metropolitan areas are still not in compliance with the clean air standards.

benefits of tighter controls. Their arguments were usually accepted by political representatives in state governments and the U.S. Congress. Constant pressure was placed on state and federal regulators to refrain from strict enforcement of the clean air rules.

Similarly, automotive companies, which had installed technology to reduce pollution from vehicle tailpipes only after fierce resistance, lobbied long, hard, and successfully against any strengthening of clean air standards or requirements that cars and trucks be more efficient in their use of fuel.

Meanwhile, evidence had been slowly accumulating on the effects of acid precipitation and other air pollution on natural systems in North America. Long-term research at the Hubbard Brook Experimental Forest in New Hampshire conducted by Gene E. Likens and F. Herbert Bormann starting in the late 1960s systematically examined the complex interactions among land, air, and water, and their impact on ecological systems. By the early 1970s this research was turning up evidence of a correlation between acid deposition from air and acidified fresh water in the study area, as well as a decline in soil nutrients. Research in Canada during this period began to suggest that air pollution carried over long distances, including pollution from the United States, was acidifying lakes and streams and harming freshwater life in Quebec Province and other parts of Canada. From Europe, re-

...the NAPAP program was a perfect excuse for doing nothing in the face of mounting evidence of the widespread harm caused by acid rain and air pollution transported over long distances.

ports were coming in of a frightening new phenomenon—*Waldsterben*, the death of the forest. Vast acreages of woodland in central Europe were dying because of air pollution in that heavily industrialized sector of the world.

In the United States, however, the response of policy makers was that there was too much scientific uncertainty to undertake what they invariably described as a very costly new program to control the emissions and transport of pollution that was causing acid rain. The politicians were reinforced by a stream of information provided by industry scientists, including scientists of the Edison Electric Institute, the trade group of the electric utility industry, which stressed the uncertainties and minimized the damage that air pollution was causing the natural environment, human health, and man-made structures. As a result, Congress voted in 1980 to create the National Acid Precipitation Assessment Program (often abbreviated as NAPAP), a 10-year study ostensibly intended to remove the scientific uncertainties and provide a reliable road map for action.

As Gene Likens has described it, "The NAPAP effort was 'big' science on a forced march, with platoons of consultants, civil servants and scientists stepping to the cadence of a federal bureaucracy." For the extremely conservative administration of Ronald Reagan, which came to power in 1981 with the prime objective of lifting the regulatory burden on industry, particularly environmental regulation, the NAPAP program was a perfect excuse for doing nothing in the face of mounting evidence of the widespread harm caused by acid rain and air pollution transported over long distances. Administration officials used preliminary reports from the study to cast doubt on the seriousness of the problem. David Stockman, the first head of Reagan's Office of Management and Budget, whose mission was to chop away at the reach of government, stated that air pollution controls were already too stringent and that there was no need for any action to cope with acid rain. Such pollution, he told a group of businessmen, affected only a few fish in a few lakes in the Adirondacks.

As my co-essayist in this book, Orie L. Loucks, commented in an assessment of the NAPAP process, "The Reagan administration's approach to NAPAP in 1981 and 1982 was designed to delay and contain development of new knowledge. An apparent goal was to have the scientific assessments support a pre-determined decision: to postpone action on acid-gas emissions controls." That goal was maintained by the Reagan Administration throughout its term of office, although it was tempered to some degree when William D. Ruckelshaus replaced Anne Burford as head of the Environmental Protection Agency (EPA).

Evidence of the damage being wrought by air pollution transported long distances through the atmosphere continued to accumulate. The Canadian government, alarmed by the decline of their lakes and by reports of widespread damage to sugar maples, pressed Washington hard to act on acid rain. The issue became a central irritant in relations between the two governments as the White House declined to act despite repeated assurances it would. Yet by 1986, a cautiously worded report by the National Academy of Sciences, which generally speaks for mainstream science in the United States, pointed unmistakably to the

Ashland oil refinery, Elizabeth, Pennsylvania

relationship between airborne sulfur and nitrogen pollutants and the acidification of fresh water in parts of the country.

The report also noted a decline in tree ring growth in the eastern United States and increased mortality of red spruces at high elevations, although it concluded there were not enough data to link those trends with acid precipitation or other air pollution. Before then, the issue of forest damage had been largely ignored by the NAPAP process and in the debate over the policy response to air pollution. While considerable research on forest effects was thenceforward included as part of the NAPAP agenda, it became perhaps the most politicized and deceptively treated issue in the entire acid rain debate.

In fact, scientific data on the effects of air pollution on trees had been building up in this country since at least the 1960s with the long-term research of Dr. Hubert Vogelmann and his colleagues at Camels Hump in the Green Mountains of Vermont. Their studies found a high incidence of dying red spruce at higher altitudes and a slower growth rate among these trees, and some decline among other species, including birch and maple. Further research suggested that acidification was preventing nutrients from being absorbed by tree roots because it released aluminum in the soil and destroyed the microorganisms attached to the roots and required for absorption. Meanwhile, reports were coming in of forest decline in ecological systems other than high elevations along the eastern seaboard. Orie Loucks was finding evidence of heavy concentrations of acid deposition in the Ohio Valley and of disastrous levels of tree death and decline in the hardwoods in the broad region known as the mixed mesophytic forest. From the South came reports of a significant decline in tree ring growth in the commercial yellow pine plantations.

...big forest products corporations were worried much more about what would happen to the value of their equity if the stock markets concluded that their major asset was being depleted by pollution.

In the mid-1980s, I traveled to Raleigh, North Carolina, to visit Dr. Robert Bruck, a scientist who was examining the interrelationship of atmospheric chemistry and tree health at the top of Mt. Mitchell, the tallest peak on the eastern seaboard. Bruck was finding a surprising number of dead and dying red spruce and Fraser fir trees, very high levels of acid precipitation, and dense concentrations of volatile organic chemicals in the atmosphere. The air pollution on the remote mountain was at levels usually found in centers of heavy industrial and urban activity. Bruck was also finding leaf damage and the destruction of the root microorganisms in the soil. Bruck said at the time that there were many possible explanations of what was happening on the mountain, but that most probably air pollution was playing an important role.

Mt. Mitchell was under snow and not accessible during that visit, but I returned a couple of years later and met Bruck at the top of the mountain. The crest looked shockingly like a World War I battlefield. As far as the eye could see along the ridge were dead trees, mostly Fraser firs. All around were also dead and dying spruce trees. The ground was covered with nothing but blackberry and other coarse brush. Farther down the mountain, Bruck pointed to a hollow where more trees were dying, some of them hardwoods. As a result of the air pollution readings and the results of his research team's study of leaf effects and soil chemistry, Bruck was now much surer that pollution was playing a central role in the accelerating decline of the trees on Mt. Mitchell, probably making them more vulnerable to disease and other natural afflictions. The trees, he believed, were cooking in a thick soup of acid and ozone.

Despite all the evidence correlating widespread forest damage with the steep increase in air pollution in the post-World War II era, industry and many government scientists remained in a state of denial about the crisis into the 1990s—and indeed, many still do to this day. Unwilling to pay the cost of reducing the destructive emissions from power plants and auto vehicles, industry invested instead in producing evidence that cast doubt on the emerging science and in lobbying activities to prevent effective government action. One of the better-financed groups lobbying against a strengthened Clean Air Act in the mid-1980s was a group called Citizens for Sensible Control of Acid Rain. Upon inspection, the group turned out not to be a citizens' group at all as the term is generally used, but a lobbying organization financed by coal and power companies and run by a public relations firm that spent millions of dollars to generate mail opposing controls, alleging that controls would increase utility bills by 30 percent.

Even the forest products industry, whose commercial tree plantations were at risk from air pollution, maintained a posture of denial that anything was amiss. This seeming unwillingness to act to protect its assets puzzled me for some time until a timber company executive provided an off-the-record explanation. Yes, he said, the industry was worried about the deterioration of its stock of standing timber. But the big forest products corporations were worried much more about what would happen to the value of their equity if the stock markets concluded that their major asset was being depleted by pollution. Private foresters, joined in a number of instances by U.S. Forest Service scientists, insisted that there was no widespread damage to trees and what little there was could be explained by insect damage, drought, disease, freezing temperatures—anything but air pollution.

Meanwhile, the NAPAP process continued with all deliberate (and dilatory) speed. As Gene Likens noted, it produced some excellent science and some questionable science. Some of the directors of the program were capable public servants seeking the truth; others were seen as serving the Reagan Administration's delaying game. In September 1987, the program issued its long-awaited interim report. The executive summary of the report prepared by the NAPAP staff said that little evidence had been found to suggest any immediate broad threat to the environment or public health from acid rain, and that "a significant increase in the number of acidic lakes is unlikely over the next few decades." It also said that little damage to forests had been found, none to crops, and there were "no demonstrated effects on human health."

The executive director of NAPAP at the time, J. Laurence Kulp, a former science professor at Columbia University who later worked as a scientist for the Weyerhaeuser timber company, said in presenting the report to the news media that it was a "state-of-the-science document," and "not a policy document at all." But the conclusions of the executive summary drew unusually sharp criticism from a number of scientists engaged in the issue. Gene Likens, for example, told the *New*

York Times, "I was disappointed because the executive summary really misrepresents the scientific understanding about the effects of acid deposition on the environment." He particularly pointed to the report's failure to consider the effects of acid rain on tree foliage. "To say there is no effect is just not true," he stated. Eville Gorham, a professor of ecology at the University of Minnesota, complained that the report "conveys no sense of urgency but instead provides a rationale for ongoing research without any sense that controls may be needed."

Only 31 lines of the massive study were devoted to the deterioration of forests in the South...

By the end of the Reagan era, however, momentum for controlling acid rain and other air pollution mounted sharply, despite the administration's continuing effort to minimize the problem. Scientific evidence of the causes and effects of pollution on natural resources could no longer be brushed aside, and the environmental community and the public were demanding action. Politicians began to respond to the pressure. A group of eastern state governments filed suit to force the federal government to impose controls. In a telling illustration of the changing political climate, the governor of New York State, an area that was a major recipient of air pollution carried from the west, and the governor of Ohio, a state in which large quantities of the pollution originated, joined to propose a plan for curbing acid rain.

By the election campaign of 1988, Republican presidential candidate George Bush was promising that he would be the "environmental president" if elected and would press Congress to improve the Clean Air Act, including action to control acid rain. Despite fierce resistance from within his own administration, including rearguard holding actions by his chief of staff and the director of his Office of Management and Budget, Bush followed through on his campaign promise after his election, and sent legislation to Congress.

The 10-year NAPAP study program, meanwhile, ground noisily to its conclusion. Issued early in 1991, the final report filled 28 volumes and some 6,000 pages. Its cost was more than half a billion dollars. In summary, the report found that while acid rain had caused some environmental damage, it was far less than that initially feared. A *New York Times* story on the report carried a headline stating, "Worst Fears on Acid Rain Unrealized." Dr. James R. Mahoney, director of the program at the time, said that the findings showed that "the amount of damage is less than we once thought, and it's much less than some of the characterizations we sometimes hear." The summary of the report was particularly sanguine about the impact of air pollution on forests, stating that "The vast majority of forests in the United States are not affected by decline."

The report, especially the conclusions reached by those in charge of its publication, produced a torrent of criticism from scientists who reviewed it. They noted that some of the compelling scientific evidence of the effects of pollution on trees, including Dr. Bruck's research on Mt. Mitchell, was not included in the report. Only 31 lines of the massive study were devoted to the deterioration of forests in the South, and relatively little attention was paid to the decline of hardwoods in the East. Several scientists complained that the report did not deal adequately with the issue of how acid deposition might be affecting nutrients in the soil. In general the critics felt that the report's conclusion that the forests were not affected by air pollution was a misstatement of the evidence and that the most that could be said was that the research did not yet show signs of widespread stress and mortality.

Industry seized on the report in its efforts to water down the pending legislation to strengthen the Clean Air Act. The Edison Electric Institute, for example, commented that the report showed that acid rain was causing less damage than anticipated and lent credence to its argument that industry should be given more "flexibility" in dealing with air pollution.

However, Congress paid virtually no attention to the NAPAP study as it completed its action on clean air legislation. In 1990, after a long, often contentious debate, it significantly strengthened the law with a series of far-ranging amendments, including provisions to sharply reduce sulfur emissions and other precursors of acid rain. Included was an innovative, if controversial, provision to permit trading of sulfur pollution "credits" which would use the marketplace in reaching the goal of reducing the nation's sulfur emissions by half by the year 2000.

By the end of 1994, according to the EPA, sulfur dioxide emissions nationwide were down 25 percent and virtually every other air pollutant, including smog, had also fallen by at least several percentage points. Sulfur polluting permits were trading on the open market at a fraction of what had been estimated when the measure was adopted—demonstrating that utilities and other polluters could reduce their pollution at a far lower cost than they had been predicting during the legislative debate. It appeared that the target of cutting sulfur emissions in half by 2000 would be easily attained. The threat to the forests of Appalachia was ebbing.

...the tragedy of the forests will only deepen without a major, sustained, and meaningful response.

Or was it?

I n an April 1996 issue of the authoritative journal *Science*, Gene Likens and his colleagues at the Hubbard Brook Experimental Forest published an article summarizing their data on the long-term effects of acid rain on the forest ecosystem. They found that the forest remained "much more susceptible" to acid deposition from the air than expected, and that while damage to forests might be reversible, the recovery process would be very slow. "A major policy implication of this analysis is that the 1990 amendments to the Clean Air Act *will not be adequate* to protect surface waters and forest soils of the northeastern United States against further anthropogenic acidification." Likens subsequently told a reporter that "The whole issue of acid rain has literally fallen from public view. The public thinks the problem has been solved, and I would suggest to you that it has not been solved."

In North Carolina, Bob Bruck reported in early 1997 that the spruce and fir ecosystems at the top of Mt. Mitchell had collapsed and that trees were dying all the way down the sides of the mountain. A recently completed study by federal and state scientists had found the southern Appalachian region to be still afflicted with high levels of acid deposition. Ozone pollution in 1996 had been the highest in history, he noted. Visibility from the mountain on a summer day is often only 9 miles compared to 70 miles 25 years ago.

The Clean Air Act amendments did not fix the problem for Appalachia, Bruck said. "We put a band-aid on it a thousand miles away. The old, dirty power plants that are causing our problem are buying pollution credits from utilities in Idaho and Wyoming where they don't have a pollution problem" and continuing to contribute to the soup of pollution in Appalachia's air. Industry and conservative politicians, he contended, are using the excuse of scientific uncertainty to insist that the markets regulate pollution. "It's the greatest smoke and mirrors exercise in history."

Following the annual Lucy Braun Association forest conference in Charleston, West Virginia, in 1996, scientists and other participants issued a statement noting that they had reached "unprecedented agreement that eastern U.S. forests have been placed at risk due to air pollution in combination with natural stresses." At that meeting Gerard Hertel, assistant director for forest health of the U.S. Forest Service, stressed that more emphasis needed to be put on the impact of acid deposition and ozone on trees, forests, and forest ecosystems.

Clearly, industry and government policy makers failed to end the airborne assault on Appalachia's forests. And now there are other grave threats to the trees that suggest that the tragedy of the forests will only deepen without a major, sustained, and meaningful response.

One of the threats is global warming. The carbon dioxide from the burning of fossil fuels and other gases released by human activity is accumulating in the atmosphere, and, according to the most credible scientific consensus, preventing heat from the sun from escaping out of the earth's atmosphere. If this trend is not reversed, the consensus holds, the earth's temperature could rise quickly and substantially—a global average of between 3 and 8 degrees Fahrenheit—in the next century. This significant rise in temperature at unprecedented speed would have a profound impact on natural systems, especially on forests, which are unable to adjust quickly. Added to the pressures already ravaging the trees of Appalachia, this change of climate could have a devastating effect on the region.

There is also evidence that ultraviolet radiation from the sun, which is reaching the earth's surface with increasing intensity because the protective shield of stratospheric ozone has been thinned by man-made chlorofluorocarbons and other industrial chemicals, is inflicting heavy damage on tree foliage, particularly the needles of evergreens.

Recently, timber companies have added a new insult to the trees and people of Appalachia. Chipping mills, which turn standing trees into fodder for making pulp, have been rapidly spreading up from the South. These mills clearcut the forests within a radius of 60 miles around them, including not only mature trees but saplings and branches, to feed the hungry maws of their chipping machines. "People are very upset about it around here, but they are so used to big corporations raping their land they feel they can't do anything about it," said Doug Murray, a local activist trying to protect the

Tulip tree leaf showing signs of UV-B damage

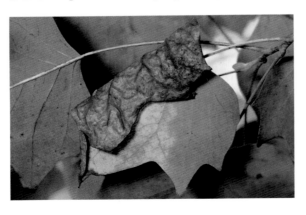

Bowater Paper and Pulp
plant, Calhoun, Tennessee

forests of his native Campbell County, Kentucky.

It is time—well past time—for their fellow citizens across the
country to join with the people of Appalachia to help them protect
their land and their trees, their health and their livelihood. It is time
that ways are found for the region to achieve a measure of prosperity
that does not entail raping the land and its resources.

And there is much that can and should be done.

First, the pollution that is killing the trees of Appalachia must be
slashed far below current levels. It is not enough to reduce national
emissions of sulfur by 50 percent if too much of the remaining pollution
continues to fall as acid rain on this beleaguered region. Hydrocarbons
and volatile organic gases from motor vehicles and industry also must
be sharply reduced. Regulations to reduce ozone levels proposed by the
Environmental Protection Agency will help, but not nearly enough. It is
clear that more than additional band-aids will be necessary.

Some further progress can be made by installing additional scrubbers in power plant stacks, requiring the burning of cleaner fuel, tamp-
ing down still more on tailpipe emissions, and enforcing existing clean
air regulations more vigorously. But these efforts can at best keep pace
with the additional pollution produced by a growing population and a
growing economy. Far more fundamental, far-reaching changes will be
needed in the way we live and work if we are to protect the forests of
Appalachia and in so doing serve our own well-being and the health
of the planet.

Quite clearly there must be a change in the kind of energy we use,
the way we use it, and how we look at its costs. Most of the air pollution that is killing the trees, as well as harming the hearts and lungs of

many of our citizens and causing a potentially disruptive change in the earth's climate, comes from fossil fuels—chiefly coal and oil. These fuels were the foundation of the industrial and technological revolutions. They made possible the standard of living Americans and people of other industrialized countries enjoy. By now, however, we have learned the high price we are paying for that standard of living in terms of our environment, our health, and the deterioration of the things we build. We have also learned that there are alternatives to the way we use energy today that would enable us to sustain a high standard of living without the toll now being exacted on the natural world.

Certainly we can substantially reduce the amount of fossil fuels we burn and the pollution we produce by using energy more efficiently. Although the gap has narrowed in recent years, industry in western Europe and Japan still uses far less energy per unit of produc-

Coal loading docks, Dupont & Occidental chemical plant, Kanawha River, Marmett, West Virginia

tion. American industry could substantially improve its competitiveness in international markets by reducing its energy costs while producing less pollution. We can also be more efficient in the way we drive. Technology already available could let us drive at least twice as many miles per gallon of gasoline.

In early 1997 a statement on climate change signed by over 2000 economists, including six Nobel laureates, called for steps to be taken to reduce the pollution that is causing global warming. Such steps, including a tax on carbon dioxide emissions, the chief greenhouse gas, could produce benefits that would outweigh the costs. A growing number of thoughtful scientists and economists, as well as environmentalists, are calling for taxes on fossil fuels to discourage their use, with the proceeds being used to lower taxes on wages and capital.

Such taxes can help reveal the true cost of burning fossil fuel, which is far more than we pay for our electricity or at the gasoline pump or for the manufactured products we buy Those price tags still do not reflect the cost of hospitalization and other health care for those sickened by pollution; the lost days of work and lower productivity of unhealthy workers; of the repairs and repainting that must be done to buildings; the cost of maintaining armed forces to protect sources of oil in faraway lands; the cost of poisoned streams and barren, stripped hills left behind by exhausted coal mines; of beautiful estuaries and bays fouled by oil; of the loss of crops; of wildlife; of trees and forests.

Such a heavy price simply cannot be sustained. The age of fossil fuels clearly is approaching its final stage. Alternatives such as solar energy already are available, awaiting only a welcoming economic context to be deployed across the globe. But fierce resistance by stubborn, entrenched, rich and powerful vested interests, including the energy and utility industries and the auto makers, are impeding the transition to an age of cleaner energy.

This rearguard resistance will only make the transition more costly and difficult in the long run. But it is succeeding because the American people apparently accept the lies of the polluters. Unaware of the enormous stakes for themselves and their children, they are still unwilling to bear the short-term costs and make the life-style changes necessary to kick the fossil fuel habit. If our culture continues to be characterized by rampant individualism that, to cite one example, forgoes public transportation and impels us to drive one by one to work in gas-guzzling cars, then the forests of Appalachia, and eventually the rest of the country, will continue to decline. If our lives continue to be dominated by rampant consumerism that measures success by the accumulation of ever more material possessions, we will lose not only the trees but ourselves.

This nation, which has neglected Appalachia for so long, owes it to the region to ...care for the trees, the land, and the people.

Finally, if the forests of Appalachia are to be saved, the nation must care for the people of Appalachia. By now it is widely recognized that environmental degradation is often a symptom of poverty. People who are poor usually lack the political power to resist the polluters, the resource exploiters, the degraders of the land. Over the long haul, the Appalachian landscape cannot be protected unless there are decent jobs for the workers, adequate housing for their families, good schools for their children, and communities that encourage their residents to care about their fellow-citizens and the land they inhabit together.

This nation, which has neglected Appalachia for so long, owes it to the region to provide the assistance necessary to care for the trees, the land, and the people. If coal mining and timbering are no longer viable or desirable, and if a return to an agrarian economy is no longer possible, help must be provided to stimulate alternatives. Tourism and recreation are already major contributors to wide areas of Appalachia and much can be done to develop those industries. There can be substantial, useful, and economically rewarding long-term employment in restoring the forests, the depleted soils, the degraded streams, and the abandoned industrial areas of the region. In the emerging economy built on information and communication, there will be no reason the once-isolated hills and valleys of Appalachia cannot be fully integrated into the mainstream of America's economic life. But it will not happen unless Americans are willing to lend a helping hand to their fellow-citizens in that long-suffering region.

Appalachia's forests can still be saved and rejuvenated, their beauty and their utility restored, if the American people respond before it is too late.

But time is running out. The trees are still dying.

An Appreciation

This book has been brought to publication through a generous gift made in honor of Harry and 'Becca Dalton by their loving children. Harry Dalton is founder of the Sierra Club's Southern Appalachian Ecoregion Task Force.

The publisher, editors, and authors of this book are grateful for the support of the Dalton family and for their continuing dedication to the protection of the magnificent forests of the Appalachian region.

Contributors

Harvard Ayers, author of the foreword to *An Appalachian Tragedy* and co-editor, is Professor of Anthropology and Sustainable Development at Appalachian State University in Boone, North Carolina. He is an officer in the Southern Appalachian Mountain Initiative, an eight-state government-private effort to solve air pollution problems in the region. He is also director of the Northern Hardwood Damage Survey, a scientific research project being conducted in the high-elevation woodlands of North Carolina, Virginia, and Tennessee.

Chris Bolgiano, whose essay "Communities in Crisis" begins on page 116, is a freelance journalist and author. She lives in the Appalachian mountains of Virginia where she took up rural residence during the back-to-the-land movement in the 1970s. Her articles have appeared in the *New York Times, Washington Post, Audubon, American Forests*, and other magazines. Her first book, *Mountain Lion: An Unnatural History of Pumas and People*, was published (Stackpole) in 1995. She is currently at work on a book about the natural and cultural histories of Appalachia.

William B. Grant, who prepared the comprehensive scientific bibliography in the appendix, is a senior research scientist in the Atmospheric Sciences Division of the National Aeronautical and Space Administration. As a physicist he has also held research positions at SRI International in Menlo Park and at the Jet Propulsion Laboratory in Pasadena, California. When not working at NASA, he conducts research on the effects of air pollution on forests, among other interests. He is Air Quality Chair of the Virginia Chapter of the Sierra Club.

Jenny Hager, co-editor and photographer for *An Appalachian Tragedy*, is a freelance photojournalist specializing in travel, nature, and environmental issues. She has been on photographic expeditions to Denali, the Himalayas, and the Alps, as well as most parts of the United States. Prior to becoming a professional photographer, she was a mountaineer and teacher of wilderness survival skills. She established her firm, Alpine Images, in 1984 and since then her photographs have been widely published, notably by Abbeville Press, *Audubon, Der Spiegel, Geo, Harper's, Landscape Architecture, National Geographic World, Newsweek, Outside*, Sierra Club Books, *Time*, and *U.S. News & World Report*.

Mary Hufford has been a folklife specialist at the American Folklife Center of the Library of Congress for the past 15 years. Her essay "Weathering the Storm," beginning on page 146, is drawn from her work on the Appalachian Forest Folklife

Project, a documentary study funded by the Lila Wallace Reader's Digest Community Folklife Program. Among her monographs are *Chaseworld: Foxhunting and Storytelling in New Jersey's Pine Barrens;* *One Space, Many Places: Folklife and Land Use Planning in New Jersey's Pinelands National Reserve;* and an edited collection of essays, *Conserving Culture: A New Discourse on Heritage.* Her essays on culture and environment have appeared in *Folklife Center News, American Forests,* and *Orion Magazine.*

Charles E. Little is a co-editor and wrote the chapter introductions and captions for *An Appalachian Tragedy.* Formerly head of natural resources policy analysis at the Congressional Research Service and president of the American Land Forum, an environmental policy think tank, he has been a full-time writer since 1986. Among his most recent books are *Discover America* (Smithsonian) and *The Dying of the Trees* (Viking). The latter, now in paperback (Penguin, 1997), was a finalist for a *Los Angeles Times* Book Prize.

Orie L. Loucks, author of the essay in Chapter 2, holds the position of Ohio Eminent Scholar in Applied Ecosystem Studies and Professor of Zoology at Miami University, Oxford, Ohio. He taught plant ecology at the University of Wisconsin from 1972 to 1978; in 1978 he joined The Institute of Ecology in Indianapolis as science director, heading studies concerning the regional effects of air pollutants and acidic deposition; he became director of the Holcomb Research Institute at Butler University in 1983. He has published some 200 scientific papers and reports on ecology, ecosystem studies, and pollution effects in both aquatic and terrestrial systems. He was a member of the Board of Governors of The Nature Conservancy for ten years (1984–94) and a member of the National Academy of Sciences Board on Water Science and Technology, among other positions. He is founder and chair of the Lucy Braun Association for the Mixed Mesophytic Forest and serves on the board of the Cincinnati Museum of Natural History.

Philip Shabecoff, who wrote the essay "After Decades of Deception, a Time to Act" (page 184), was a reporter for the *New York Times* for 32 years before becoming founding publisher of Greenwire, the daily environmental news service. He is the author of two books on environmental history and policy and is currently writing a book about the future of the environmental movement.

Tom Suzuki, designer and art director for *An Appalachian Tragedy,* heads his own graphic design firm specializing in magazines, books, and other publications. Before establishing his firm in 1982,

he was art director for Time-Life Books. During his tenure, Time-Life Books published more than 200 titles. For the past 20 years he has been a faculty member of the Stanford University Alumni Association's Professional Publishing Course.

T. H. Watkins, whose essay "The View from Brasstown Bald" begins on page 40, has written nearly 300 articles and reviews for more than 50 publications and is the author of 25 books. His *Righteous Pilgrim*, a biography of Harold L. Ickes, FDR's Interior Secretary, was winner of a *Los Angeles Times* Book Prize and finalist for both the National Book Award and the National Book Critics Circle Award. Formerly senior editor of *American Heritage* magazine and editor (1982–96) of *Wilderness* magazine, he is at present the Wallace Stegner Professor of American Studies at Montana State University.

Picture Credits

All photographs are by Jenny Hager except the following:

Legend:
L left; R right; T top; C center; B bottom

Along the Spine of Time
p.14T Paul Rezendes; 14B Hugh Morton;
15T Daniel J. Cox/Natural Exposures;
15C & B Bill Lea; 24 Lyntha Eiler; 25 Lyntha
Eiler; 26–27 Terry Eiler; 27T Jane Beck/Vermont
Folklife Center; 27B Lyntha Eiler; 28 Paul
Rezendes; 29T & BL Jerry LeBlond; 31 Lyntha
Eiler; 33BR Steve Kaufman; 35T & R Terry Eiler;
36 Lyntha Eiler

The Appalachians' Last Stand
p. 77BR Quintin McClellan, Virginia Tech;
80–81 Shenandoah National Park Service

The Broken Web of Life
p. 103T Bates Littlehales; 103C Harry Ellis;
107C & B Harry Ellis; 111T Maslowski Wildlife
Productions; 111BL Bill Lea; 113CB Hugh
Morton; 113B Connie Toops; 126–127 Lyntha
Eiler; 128–129 Lyntha Eiler; 130–131 Lyntha
Eiler; 132TL ,TR, B Terry Eiler; 132–133 Lyntha
Eiler; 134 Lyntha Eiler; 135 Lyntha Eiler;
136–137 Richard Alexander Cooke III; 137TR
Terry Eiler; 139T Richard Alexander Cooke III;
139BL Steve Kaufman; 139BR Jerry LeBlond;
144–145 Lyntha Eiler

A Culture at Risk
Photographs courtesy of the American Folklife
Center, Library of Congress. Special thanks are
due the center for use of photographs from their
collection for this part of the book, especially
those taken by Lyntha and Terry Eiler. The
photographs are among those made possible
through a generous grant from the Lila Wallace
Reader's Digest Community Folklife Program
administered through the Fund for Folk Culture.

Weathering the Storm
Photographs by Lyntha Eiler

Concerned Organizations and Government Agencies

Those who wish to pursue some of the issues raised in this book are encouraged to contact organizations listed here for further information. The private, non-profit groups are shown first and are a good place to start. Also listed are the two largest units of the national park system in the region, the National Forest offices, and two state park and forest offices.

Nonprofit, Public-Interest Organizations

The twenty organizations listed here by no means represent the total number of civic, educational, and scientific groups at work in the Appalachian forests on air pollution and other issues. Indeed, some of the most effective of these groups are not listed here since there are so many and since their focus is most often relatively narrow and somewhat outside the range of issues dealt with in this book. Still, the citizen-activist may find the smaller groups the best venue for forceful advocacy. The best way to find out about them is to begin with larger organizations and work down.

Acid Rain Foundation
1509 Varsity Drive
Raleigh, NC 27606
(919) 515-3311
Strives to foster a greater understanding of air quality issues, including acid rain, air pollutants, and global climate change, and to help bring about solutions. To achieve these goals, the foundation focuses on public awareness and provides educational resources to a wide range of audiences.

American Forests
1516 P St. NW
Washington, DC 20005
(202) 667-3300
Seeks to maintain and improve the heath and value of trees and forests. Its quarterly magazine, *American Forests*, covers all issues relating to forest health, including air pollution.

Appalachian Mountain Club
5 Joy St.
Boston, MA 02108
(617) 523-0636
Publishes *Appalachia Journal*, *AMC Outdoors*, AMC guidebooks. The club is interested in conservation policy, environmental research, and education as it relates to recreation in northern Appalachian forests and parks.

Appalachian Trail Conference
P.O. Box 807
Harpers Ferry, WV 25425
(304) 535-6331
Publishes guidebooks and organizes the management and preservation of the entire Appalachian Trail, from Maine to Georgia.

Clean Air Network
1200 New York Ave. NW #400
Washington, DC 20005
(202) 289-2429
A national alliance of more than 900 local, state, and national citizen organizations working to protect air quality. The network's goal is to increase public support and awareness of clean air measures using public education, media, and grassroots organizing efforts to influence policy and implement and enforce relevant laws. The network focuses on human effects of air pollution, but also looks at air pollution's effects on forests. Publication: *Clean Air at the Crossroads: Progress Made and Challenges*.

Greenpeace
1436 U St. NW
Washington, DC 20009
(202) 462-1177
Air pollution due to toxic releases, such as those by incinerators, is a major focus. Greenpeace's toxics campaign informs the public about health dangers and publishes informative reports. See especially *Playing with Fire: Hazardous Waste Incineration*.

The Lucy Braun Association
c/o Dr. Orie L. Loucks
Department of Zoology
Miami University
Oxford, OH 45056
(513) 529-1677
An organization of scientists and citizens concerned with conserving the mixed mesophytic forest, which stretches from Alabama to Pennsylvania along the west-facing slopes, plateaus, coves, and hollows of the Appalachian chain. The association's purpose is to expand public appreciation for the beauty, antiquity, and unmatched diversity of the forest, and to work for programs to prevent its decline. Publications include *Tree Mortality in the Mixed Mesophytic Forest: 1994-1996 Survey Results*, *Appalachia Forest Action Project*, and *News from the Mother Forest*, a newsletter.

National Audubon Society
1901 Pennsylvania Ave. NW
Washington, DC 20006
(202) 861-2242
The NAS Forest Habitat Campaign seeks to sustain and restore America's forest ecosystems and the habitat they provide to birds and wildlife through informed grassroots activism backed by sound science. Audubon has a long history of supporting ecologically appropriate forest protection and restoration.

National Parks and Conservation Association
1176 Massachusetts Ave. NW
Washington, DC 20036
(202) 223-6722
Dedicated solely to preserving, protecting, and enhancing the U.S. national park system, NPCA focuses on the health of the entire system as well as the processes of planning, management, and evaluation for specific sites and programs. The southeast regional office has been involved in air pollution in the Great Smoky Mountains National Park. Publications: *National Parks* magazine; *ParkWatcher*.

National Wildlife Federation
Laurel Ridge Conservation Education Center
8925 Leesburg Pike
Vienna, VA 22184
(703) 790-4000
Assists individuals and organizations in conserving wildlife and other natural resources. NWF's Northeast Natural Resource Center in Montpelier, Vermont, works to protect the great "Northern Forest," which extends from the Adirondacks to northern Maine.

Ozone Action
1621 Connecticut Ave. NW
Washington, DC 20009
(202) 265-6738
Works exclusively on atmospheric issues: ozone depletion and climate change. The organization answers daily media and public inquiries and provides analysis of the latest scientific and policy developments on atmospheric issues. Publishes informative reports and fact sheets, including *Environmental Effects of Ozone Depletion* and *Deadly Complacency: US CFC Production, the Black Market, and Ozone Depletion*.

Potomac Appalachian Trail Club
118 Park St. SE
Vienna, VA 22180
(703) 242-0693
Members of the club maintain 240 miles of the Appalachian Trail from Virginia to Pennsylvania. Publishes maps and guidebooks of the Appalachian Trail. Members also construct and maintain shelters and cabins on the trail.

Sierra Club
Southern Appalachian Highlands
Ecoregion Task Force
Route 7 Box 183
Boone, NC 28607
(704) 262-6381
The task force works to instill pride in the natural and cultural environment of the southern Appalachian region. Conducts research, disseminates information, and increases public awareness of the impacts of air pollution on the forests of the region. To hold government officials responsible for what is happening to the forests, the task force organizes fly-overs and field trips to areas where die-back is occurring. Publishes a bimonthly tabloid-sized newspaper, *Appalachian Voice.*

Southern Environmental Law Center
201 W. Main St., #14
Charlottesville, VA 22902
(804) 977-4040
A public interest advocacy organization, the center is committed to protecting the natural resources of the Southeast through direct advocacy in court and before regulatory agencies, through assistance to state and local environmental groups in the region, and by providing regional leadership on key southeastern environmental issues, such as forestry.

Trees for the Planet, Inc.
6407 32nd St. NW
Washington, DC 20015
(202) 362-8733
A national public interest advocacy group seeking to preserve the healthy functioning of forest ecosystems. It is currently working with the Lucy Braun Association and other groups to address forest decline in Appalachia.

Vermont Natural Resources Council
9 Bailey Ave.
Montpelier, VT 05602
(802) 223-2328
VNRC is Vermont's principal statewide environmental organization and includes more than 5,000 individuals, families, and organizations. The council focuses on protecting and restoring Vermont's rivers, streams, and wildlife; strengthening and implementing environmental laws; shaping land use and water policies; preserving Vermont's forest and agrarian heritage; and informing citzens about key issues and how to become actively involved locally and statewide. Publications: *Vermont Environmental Report, VNRC Bulletin, A Forest at Risk: The Citizens' Agenda for Saving the Northern Forest.*

Western North Carolina Alliance
70 Woodfin Place #4C
Asheville, NC 28801
(704) 258-8737
A grassroots organization, the alliance works on a variety of issues, but is mainly concerned with forests. Nine chapters and two task forces focus on forest management, sustainable foresting by private landowners, and monitoring of watersheds. Publishes a quarterly newsletter, *Accent,* and news alerts.

The Wilderness Society
900 17th St. NW
Washington, DC 20006
(202) 833-2300
Dedicated to preserving the wilderness and promoting the wise management of the nation's public lands and their resources for future generations. The Atlanta chapter has published the *Mountain Treasure* series, which identifies unprotected wildlands in Georgia, Tennessee, South Carolina, North Carolina, and Virginia.

The Wildlife Society
5410 Grosvenor Lane
Bethesda, MD 20814
(301) 897-9770
A nonprofit, scientific and educational organization of wildlife professionals; the objectives of the society are to promote sound stewardship of wildlife resources, to take an active role in preventing human-induced environmental degradation, to increase awareness and appreciation of wildlife values, and to seek the highest standards in all activities of the wildlife profession. On the topic of acid rain, the society published *Acidic Depositions: Effects on Wildlife and Habitats.*

World Resources Institute
1709 New York Ave. NW
Washington, DC 20006
(202) 638-0036
A policy research center that examines environmental and socioeconomic issues, WRI deals with such issues as forestry, air pollution, and transportation. A key WRI publication is *Air Pollution's Toll on Forests and Crops.*

National Parks

The National Park Service has been active in research on the impacts of air pollution in the Appalachians. Monitoring conducted in Great Smoky Mountains National Park, for example, has shown that air pollution transported by wind into the park has a significant negative impact on natural resources and the enjoyment of park visitors. Ground-level ozone concentrations in the park are among the highest in the eastern United States, with field surveys of vegetation conducted in 1984 identifying 90 native plant species exhibiting ozonelike foliar damage. Data collected by the Park Service from regional airports show that annual average visibility in the southern Appalachians has decreased 60 percent overall, with scenic views impaired over 90 percent of the time. The Park Service was instrumental in establishing the Southern Appalachian Mountain Initiative, a voluntary, multi-organizational program set up in 1992 to deal with the adverse effects of air pollution on southern Appalachian forests.

Great Smoky Mountains National Park
107 Park Headquarters Road
Gatlinburg, TN 37738
(423) 436-1200

Shenandoah National Park
Route 4, Box 348
Luray, VA 22835
(540) 999-2243

National Forests

Air monitoring in the region by the Forest Service includes studies of concentrations of ozone, sulfur dioxide, and nitrogen oxides. Wet and dry deposition data are collected and their effects on forest resources are monitored. Visibility conditions have been monitored using cameras, aerosol monitors, and nephelometer readings. In association with the University of New Hampshire, the White Mountain National Forest surveyed the public to rate public perception of visibility impairment. The impact of acid deposition on aquatic resources is surveyed using water chemistry studies, fish and other macroinvertebrate population data, and habitat information. Plant life is monitored through vegetation damage surveys and lichen studies indicating the species present and chemical content of the lichen tissue. Soil chemistry is also monitored. In the Daniel Boone National Forest, a study was conducted to ascertain the effects of air pollution on petroglyphs. In cooperation with other government agencies and universities, the Forest Service monitors the effect of ambient ozone concentrations on sensitive plant species, the relationship between elevation and ozone concentration, visibility impairment due to haze pollution, the effects of acid deposition on the aquatic systems, elemental composition of lichens, general health of trees in the forests, pollutants in clouds and rain water, and the effects of acid deposition on amphibian populations.

Allegheny National Forest
222 Liberty St.
P.O. Box 847
Warren, PA 16365
(814) 723-5150

Chattahoochee and Oconee National Forests
508 Oak St. NW
Gainesville, GA 30501
(770) 536-0541

Cherokee National Forest
2800 North Ocoee St. NE
P.O. Box 2010
Cleveland, TN 37320
(423) 476-9700

Daniel Boone National Forest
1700 Bypass Road
Winchester, KY 40391
(606) 745-3100

George Washington and Jefferson
National Forests
5162 Valley Pointe Parkway
Roanoke, VA 24091
(540) 265-5100

Green Mountain National Forest
Federal Building
231 N. Main
Rutland, VT 05701
(802) 747-6700

Monongahela National Forest
USDA Building
200 Sycamore St.
Elkins, WV 26241
(304) 636-1800

Croatan, Nantahala, Pisgah, and Uwharrie
National Forests
160-A Zillicoa St.
P.O. Box 2750
Asheville, NC 22801
(704) 257-4200

William B. Bankhead, Conecuh, Talladega, and
Tuskegee National Forests
2946 Chestnut St.
Montgomery, AL 36107
(334) 832-4470

Wayne National Forest
219 Columbus Road
Athens, OH 45701
(614) 592-6644

White Mountain National Forest
Federal Building
719 Main St.
Box 638
Laconia, NH 03247
(603) 528-8721

State Parks and Forests

State parks and forests are less oriented to research activities than are national park and forest units. Two that have been involved to a significant degree in the Appalachians follow.

Mt. Mitchell State Park
Route 5, Box 700
Burnsville, NC 28714
(704) 675-4611

Roan Mountain State Park
Route 1, Box 236
Roan Mountain, TN 37687
(423) 772-3303

Scientific Bibliography

Papers, reports, and books dealing with the effects of air pollution on trees and forests and associated biotic communities.

by William B. Grant

Causality

Statistics can be used to find associations between independent and dependent variables. However, associations by themselves are not sufficient to prove causality. Hill (1965) systematized the criteria that should be satisfied in biological systems for the claim of causality to be supported. These criteria include such measures of consistency as temporality and gradient; strength of association, and mechanisms, which can be step-by-step linkages; responsiveness (dose-response relationships); and plausibility, including coherence and analogy. In addition, the proposed causal agent should satisfy these criteria better than any other agent. We think that the criteria are satisfied for ozone as the cause of oak decline in the southeast United States and increased mortality for oak and hickory in the eastern United States, based on an analysis of USDA Forest Service data. Schreuder and Thomas (1991) maintain that such data were not collected to assess the effects of air pollution and so cannot be so used. We respectfully disagree.

References

Hill, A. B. (1965). The environment and disease: Association or causality? *Proceedings Royal Society of Edinburgh* 58, 295–300.

Schreuder, H. T., and C. E. Thomas (1991). Establishing cause-effect relationships using forest survey data, *Forest Science* 37, 1497–1512.

Air pollution in general

Several references cover both acid ion deposition and ozone effects.

Bibliography

Chappelka, A. H., and P. H. Freer-Smith, Predisposition of trees by air pollutants to low temperatures and moisture stress, *Environmental Pollution* 87, 105–117, 1995.

Sanders, G. E., L. Skärby, M. R. Ashmore, and J. Fuhrer, Establishing critical levels for the effects of air pollution on vegetation, *Water, Air and Soil Pollution* 85, 189–200, 1995.

Shaver, C. L., K. A. Tonnessen, and T. G. Maniero, Clearing the air at Great Smoky Mountains National Park, *Ecological Applications* 4, 690–701, 1994.

Taylor, G. E., D. W. Johnson, and C. P. Andersen, Air pollution and forest ecosystems: A regional to global perspective, *Ecological Applications* 4, 662–689, 1994.

Winner, W. E., Mechanistic analysis of plant responses to air pollution, *Ecological Applications* 4, 651–661, 1994.

Woodman, J. N., and E. B. Cowling, Airborne chemicals and forest health, *Environmental Science and Technology* 21, 120–126, 1987.

Ozone

Ozone is generally acknowledged to be the major air pollutant affecting plants in the United States. Effects on both agricultural crops and forests have been documented. Ozone in the lower atmosphere is generally formed by photochemical reactions involving hydrocarbons, oxides of nitrogen, and sunlight. Some lower-atmospheric ozone also comes from the stratosphere. The peak doses of ozone are felt in the central portion of the eastern United States, which is determined by the sources (mainly to the north) and sunlight (greater in the south). The references listed here are representative of those discussing the effects of ozone on plants. Note that while experimental studies using seedlings and saplings are easier to perform than experiments on mature trees, the results of such studies may not have much relevance to the effects on mature trees, since young trees grow faster and can generate new leaves to replace those damaged by ozone. An interesting question is why some trees, even genetic varieties of the same species, are more or less sensitive than others. The red oak family, for example, is much more sensitive to ozone than is the white oak family. It could be that the less sensitive trees have more antioxidant defenses than the more sensitive trees.

Bibliography

Chameides, W. L., P. S. Kasibhata, J. Yeinger, and H. Levy II, Growth of continental-scale metro-agro-plexes, regional ozone pollution, and world food production, *Science* 264, 74–77, 1994.

Coleman, M. D., R. E. Dickson, J. G. Isebrands, and D. F. Karnosky, Root growth and physiology of potted and field-grown trembling aspen exposed to tropospheric ozone, *Tree Physiology* 16, 145–152, 1996.

Cowling, E. B., Effects of air pollution on forests, *Journal of the Air Pollution Control Association* 35, 916–919, 1985.

de Steiguer, J. E., J. M. Pye, and C. S. Love, Air pollution damage to U.S. forests, *Journal of Forestry* 88, 17–22, 1990.

Gilliam, F. S., and N. L. Turrill, Temporal patterns of ozone pollution in West Virginia: Implications for high-elevation hardwood forests, *Journal of the Air and Waste Management Association* **45**, 621–626, 1995.

Härtling, S., and H. Schulz, Field studies of young Scots pine: Effects of air pollutants on the antioxidant system, *Fresnius Environmental Bulletin* **4**, 215–220, 1995.

Hiltbrunner, E., and W. Flückiger, Altered feeding preference of beech weevil *Rhynchaenus fagi* L. for beech foliage under ambient air pollution, *Environmental Pollution* **75**, 333–336, 1992.

Hogsett, W. E., A. Herstrom, J. A. Laurence, J. E. Weber, E. H. Lee, and D. Tingey, An approach for characterizing tropospheric ozone risk to forests, *Environmental Management* **21**, 105–120, 1997.

Jones, C. G., J. S. Coleman, and S. Findlay, Effects of ozone on interactions between plants, consumers and decomposers, in R. G. Alscher and A. Wellburn, eds., *Plant Responses to the Gaseous Environment*, Ch. 18, pp. 339–363, Chapman & Hall, London, 1994.

Karlsson, P. E., E.-L. Medin, H. Wichström, G. Selldén, G. Wallin, S. Ottosson, and L. Skärby, Ozone and drought stress—interactive effects on the growth and physiology of Norway spruce [*Picea abies* (L.) Karst.], *Water, Air and Soil Pollution* **85**, 1325–1330, 1995.

Karnosky, D. F., Z. E. Gagnon, R. E. Dickson, M.D. Coleman, E. H. Lee, and J.G. Isebrands, Changes in growth, leaf abscission, and biomass associated with seasonal tropospheric ozone exposures of *Populus tremuloides* clones and seedlings, *Canadian Journal of Forest Research* **26**, 23–37, 1996.

Kelting, D. L., J. A. Burger, and G. S. Edwards, The effects of ozone on the root dynamics of seedlings and mature red oak (*Quercus rubra* L.), *Forest Ecology and Management* **79**, 197–206, 1995.

Kley, D., H. Geiss, and V. A. Mohnen, Tropospheric ozone at elevated sites and precursor emissions in the United States and Europe, *Atmospheric Environment* **28**, 149–158, 1994.

Kobayashi, K., Variation in the relationship between ozone exposure and crop yield as derived from simple models of crop growth and ozone impact, *Atmospheric Environment* **31**, 703–714, 1997.

Lefohn, A. S., and V. C. Runeckles, Establishing standards to protect vegetation—ozone exposure/dose considerations, *Atmospheric Environment* **21**, 561–568, 1987.

Lefohn, A. S., J. A. Laurence, and R. J. Kohut, A comparison of indices that describe the relationship between exposure to ozone and reduction in the yield of agricultural crops, *Atmospheric Environment* **22**, 1229–1240, 1988.

Lefohn, A. S., D. S. Shadwick, M. C. Somerville, A. H. Chappelka, B. G. Lockaby, and R. S. Meldahl, The characterization and comparison of ozone exposure indices used in assessing the response of loblolly pine to ozone, *Atmospheric Environment* **26**A, 287–298, 1992.

Lefohn, A. S., W. Jackson, D. S. Shadwick, and H. P. Knudsen, Effect of surface ozone exposures on vegetation grown in the Southern Appalachian Mountains: Identification of possible areas of concern, *Atmospheric Environment* **31**, 1695–1708, 1997.

Legge, A. H., L. Grünhage, M. Nosal, H.-J. Jäger, and S. V. Krupa, Ambient ozone and adverse crop response: An evaluation of North American and European data as they relate to exposure indices and critical levels, *Angewandte Botanik (Goettingen)* **69**, 1192–1205, 1995.

Lucas, P. W., and J. Wolfenden, The role of plant hormones as modifiers of sensitivity to air pollutants, *Phyton* **36**, 51–56, 1996.

Maier-Maercker, U., and W. Koch, Experiments on the control capacity of stomata of *Picea abies* (L.) Karst. after fumigation with ozone and in environmentally damaged material, *Plant Cell Environment* **14**, 175–184, 1991.

Mortensen, L., A. Bastrup-Birk, and H. Ro-Poulsen, Critical levels of O_3 for wood production of European beech (*Fagus sylvatica* L.), *Water, Air and Soil Pollution* **85**, 1349–1354, 1995.

National Research Council, *Rethinking the Ozone Problem in Urban and Regional Air Pollution*, National Academy Press, Washington, DC, 1992.

Neufeld, H. S., E. H. Lee, J. R. Renfro, W. D. Hacker, and B.-H. Yu, Sensitivity of seedlings of black cherry (*Prunus serotina* Ehrh.) to ozone in Great Smoky Mountains National Park, I. Exposure-response curves for biomass, *New Phytology* **130**, 447–459, 1995.

Pääkkönen, E., J. Vahala, T. Holopainen, R. Karjalainen, and L. Kärenlampi, Growth responses and related biochemical and ultrastructural changes of the photosynthetic apparatus in birch (*Betula pendula*) saplings exposed to low concentrations of ozone, *Tree Physiology* **16**, 597–605, 1996.

Palomäki, V., S. Metsärinne, J. K. Holopainen, and T. Holopainen, The ozone sensitivity of birch (*Betula pendula*) in relation to the developmental stage of leaves, *New Phytology* **132**, 145–154, 1995.

Rebbeck, J., Chronic ozone effects on three northeastern hardwood species: Growth and biomass, *Canadian Journal of Forest Research* **26**, 1788–1798, 1996.

Reiner, S., J. J. J. Wiltshire, C. J. Wright, and J. J. Colls, The impact of ozone and drought on the water relations of ash trees (*Fraxinus excelsior* L.), *Journal of Plant Physiology* **148**, 166–171, 1996.

Renfro, J. R., Air quality monitoring and research program at Great Smoky Mountains National Park: An overview of results and findings, 65 pp., 1995.

Rosenbaum, B. J., T. C. Strickland, and M. K. McDowell, Mapping critical levels of ozone, sulfur dioxide and nitrogen dioxide for crops, forests and natural vegetation in the United States, *Water, Air and Soil Pollution* **74**, 307–319, 1994.

Samuelson, L. J., and G. S. Edwards, A comparison of sensitivity to ozone in seedlings and trees of *Quercus rubra* L., *New Phytology* **125**, 373–379, 1993.

Samuelson, L. J., J. M. Kelly, P. A. Mays, and G. S. Edwards, Growth and nutrition of *Quercus rubra* L. seedlings and mature trees after three seasons of ozone exposure, *Environmental Pollution* **91**, 317–323, 1996.

Sandermann, Jr., H., Ozone and plant health, *Annual Review of Phytopathology* **34**, 347–366, 1996.

Schmieden, U., and A. Wild, The contribution of ozone to forest decline, *Physiologia Plantarum* **94**, 371–378, 1995.

Shafer, S. R., and A. S. Heagle, Growth responses of field-grown loblolly pine to chronic doses of ozone during multiple growing seasons, *Canadian Journal of Forest Research* **19**, 821–831, 1989.

Winner, W. E., A. S. Lefohn, and I. S. Cotter, Plant responses to elevational gradients of O$_3$ exposures in Virginia, *Proceedings of the National Academy of Sciences U.S.A.* **86**, 8828–8832, 1989.

Woodbury, P. B., J. A. Laurence, and G. W. Hudler, Chronic ozone exposure alters the growth of leaves, stems and roots of hybrid *Populus*, *Environmental Pollution* **85**, 103–108, 1994.

Woodbury, P. B., J. A. Laurence, and G. W. Hudler, Chronic ozone exposure increases the susceptibility of hybrid *Populus* to disease caused by *Septoria musiva*, *Environmental Pollution* **86**, 109–114, 1994.

Acid ion deposition

Acid ion deposition is taken to mean nitrate and sulfate deposition. The deposition can be either wet, as in rain or cloud droplets, or dry, from gasses or particles. Sulfate deposition mainly serves to lower soil pH while nitrate deposition lowers pH even more and also serves as a fertilizer to stimulate growth. However, this fertilizing action is a double-edged sword, since trees receiving this extra stimulus do not put roots as deeply as they would otherwise, making them more vulnerable to periodic droughts. Nitrate also alters the nitrogen balance in the trees, making them more attractive to insects and fungal diseases. The main impact of acid ion deposition is to change the balance of trace minerals in the soil. The essential base cations (calcium, magnesium, phosphorus, and potassium) are leached from the upper soil horizons, and aluminum and transition metal ions, which are normally in the oxidized state, become more prevalent. Trees require calcium for cell structure,

magnesium for photosynthesis, and potassium for ionic conductivity. They do not require aluminum. When aluminum starts blocking the uptake of the base cations and replacing them in the tissues, tree decline begins.

Bibliography

Aber, J., K. J. Nadelhoffer, P. Steudler, and J. M. Melillo, Nitrogen saturation in northern forest ecosystems, *Bioscience* **39**, 378–386, 1989.

Aber, J. D., A. Magill, S. G. McNulty, R. D. Boone, K. J. Nadelhoffer, M. Downs, and R. Hallett, Forest biogeochemistry and primary production altered by nitrogen saturation, *Water, Air and Soil Pollution* **85**, 1665–1670, 1995.

Bondietti, E. A., N. Momoshima, W. C. Shortle, and K. T. Smith, A historical perspective on divalent cation trends in red spruce stemwood and the hypothetical relationship to acidic deposition, *Canadian Journal of Forest Research* **20**, 1850–1858, 1990.

Britton, K. O., P. Berrang, and E. Mavity, Effects of pretreatment with simulated acid rain on the severity of dogwood anthracnose, *Plant Disease* **80**, 646–649, 1996.

Brook, J. R., P. J. Samson, and S. Sillman, A meteorology-based approach to detecting the relationship between changes in SO$_2$ emission rates and precipitation concentrations of sulfate, *Journal of Applied Meteorology* **33**, 1050–1066, 1994.

Bruck, R. I., and S. R. Shafer, Effects of acid precipitation on plant diseases, in R.A. Linthurst, ed., *Direct and Indirect Effects of Acidic Deposition on Vegetation*, Ch. 3, pp. 19–32, Butterworth, Boston, 1984.

Cosby, B. J., G. M. Hornberger, J. N. Galloway, and R. F. Wright, Time scales of catchment acidification, *Environmental Science and Technology* **19**, 1144–1149, 1985.

De Vries, W., G. J. Reinds, and M. Posch, Assessment of critical loads and their exceedance on European forests using a one-layer steady-state model, *Water, Air and Soil Pollution* **72**, 357–394, 1994.

Eagar, C., and M. B. Adams, eds., *Ecology and Decline of Red Spruce in the Eastern United States*, Ecological Studies, Vol. 96, 417 pp. Springer-Verlag, New York, 1992.

Eldred, R. A., and T. A. Cahill, Trends in elemental concentrations of fine particles at remote sites in the United States, *Atmospheric Environment* **28A**, 1009–1019, 1994.

Ericsson, T., A. Göransson, H. van Oene, and G. Gobran, Interactions between aluminium, calcium and magnesium: Impacts on nutrition and growth of forest trees, *Ecological Bulletin* **44**, 191–196, 1995.

Esher, R. J., D. H. Marx, S. J. Ursic, R. L. Baker, L. R. Brown, and D. C. Coleman, Simulated acid rain effects on fine roots, ectomycorrhizae, microorganisms, and invertebrates in pine forests of the southern United States, *Water, Air and Soil Pollution* **61**, 269–278, 1992.

Fenn, M. E., M. A. Poth, and D. W. Johnson, Evidence for nitrogen saturation in the San Bernardino Mountains in Southern California, *Forest Ecology and Management* **82**, 211–236, 1996.

Gilliam, F. S., M. B. Adams, and B. M. Yurish, Ecosystem nutrient responses to chronic nitrogen inputs at Fernow Experimental Forest, West Virginia, *Canadian Journal of Forest Research* **26**, 196–205, 1996.

Heinsdorf, D., The role of nitrogen in declining Scots pine forests (*Pinus sylvestris*) in the lowland of East Germany, *Water, Air and Soil Pollution* **69**, 21–35, 1993.

Heisey, R. M., Growth trends and nutritional status of sugar maple stands on the Appalachian plateau of Pennsylvania, U.S.A., *Water, Air and Soil Pollution* **82**, 675–693, 1995.

Hendershot, W., and F. Courchesne, Effect of base cation addition on soil chemistry in a sugar maple forest of the Lower Laurentians, Quebec, *Canadian Journal of Forest Research* **24**, 609–617, 1994.

Hendershot, W., and A. R. C. Jones, Maple decline in Quebec: A discussion of possible causes and the use of fertilizers to limit damage, *Forestry Chronicle* 280–287, Aug. 1989.

Husar, R. B., J. M. Holloway, D. E. Patterson, and W. E. Wilson, Spatial and temporal pattern of eastern U.S. haziness: A summary, *Atmospheric Environment* **15**, 1919–1928, 1981.

Johnson, A. H., and T. J. Siccama, Acid deposition and forest decline, *Environmental Science and Technology* **17**, 294A–305A, 1983.

Jung, T., H. Blaschke, and P. Neumann, Isolation, identification and pathogenicity of *Phytophthora* species from declining oak stands, *European Journal of Forest Pathology* **26**, 253–272, 1996.

Kaiser, J., Acid rain's dirty business: Stealing minerals from soil, *Science* **272**, 198, 1996.

Kölling, C., and J. Prietzel, Correlations between nitrate and sulfate in the soil solution of disturbed forest ecosystems, *Biogeochemistry* **31**, 121–138, 1995.

Labandeira-Villot, X., Market instruments and the control of acid rain damage, *Energy Policy* **24**, 841–854, 1996.

Lamersdorf, N. P., and M. Meyer, Nutrient cycling and acidification of a northwest German forest site with high atmospheric nitrogen deposition, *Forest Ecology and Management* **62**, 323–354, 1993.

Lawrence, G. B., M. B. David, and W. C. Shortle, A new mechanism for calcium loss in forest-floor soils, *Nature* **378**, 162–165, 1995.

Likens, G. E., C. T. Driscoll, and D. C. Buso, Long-term effects of acid rain: Response and recovery of a forest ecosystem, *Science* **272**, 244–246, 1996.

Likens, G. E., and F. H. Bormann, Acid rain: A serious regional environmental problem, *Science* **184**, 1176–1179, 1974.

Lovett, G. M., Atmospheric deposition of nutrients and pollutants in North America: An ecological perspective, *Ecological Applications* **4**, 629–650, 1994.

Lovett, G. M., and J. G. Hubbell, Effects of ozone and acid mist on foliar leaching from eastern white pine and sugar maple, *Canadian Journal of Forest Research* **21**, 794–802, 1991.

Lynch, J. A., J. W. Grimm, and V. C. Bowersox, Trends in precipitation chemistry in the United States: A national perspective, *Atmospheric Environment* **29**, 1231–1246, 1995.

Majumdar, S. K., J. R. Halma, S. W. Cline, D. Rieker, C. Daehler, R. W. Zelnick, T. Saylor, and S. Geist, Tree ring growth and elemental concentrations in wood cores of oak species in eastern Pennsylvania: Possible influences of air pollution and acid deposition, *Environmental Technology* **12**, 41–49, 1991.

Matzner, E., and D. Murach, Soil changes induced by air pollutant deposition and their implication for forests in Central Europe, *Water, Air and Soil Pollution* **85**, 63–76, 1995.

McClure, M. S., Nitrogen fertilization of hemlock increases susceptibility to hemlock woolly adelgid, *Journal of Arboriculture* **17**, 227–230, 1991.

Ollinger, S. V., J. D. Aber, G. M. Lovett, S. E. Millham, R. G. Lathrop, and J. M. Ellis, A spatial model of atmospheric deposition for the northeastern U.S., *Ecological Applications* **3**, 459–472, 1993.

Ouimet, R., and C. Camiré, Foliar deficiencies of sugar maple stands associated with soil cation imbalances in the Quebec Appalachians, *Canadian Journal of Soil Science* **75**, 169–175, 1995.

Ouimet, R., C. Camiré, and V. Furlan, Effect of soil K, Ca, and Mg saturation and endomycorrhization on growth and nutrient uptake of sugar maple seedlings, *Plant and Soil* **179**, 207–216, 1996.

Ouimet, R., C. Camiré, and V. Furlan, Effect of soil base saturation and endomycorrhization on growth and nutrient status of sugar maple seedlings, *Canadian Journal of Soil Science* **76**, 109–115, 1996.

Pääkkönen, E., and T. Holopainen, Influence of nitrogen supply on the response of clones of birch (*Betula pendula* Roth.) to ozone, *New Phytology* **129**, 595–603, 1995.

Pardo, L. H., and C. T. Driscoll, Critical loads for nitrogen deposition: Case studies at two northern hardwood forests, *Water, Air and Soil Pollution* **89**, 105–128, 1996.

Payette, S., M.-J. Fortin, and C. Morneau, The recent sugar maple decline in southern Quebec: Probable causes deduced from tree rings, *Canadian Journal of Forest Research* **26**, 1069–1078, 1996.

Pearson, J., and A. Soares, A hypothesis of plant susceptibility to atmospheric pollution based on intrinsic nitrogen metabolism: Why acidity really is the problem, *Water, Air and Soil Pollution* **85**, 1227–1232, 1995.

Persson, H., and H. Majdi, Effects of acid deposition on tree roots in Swedish forest stands, *Water, Air and Soil Pollution* **85**, 1287–1292, 1995.

Persson, H., H. Majdi, and A. Clemensson-Lindell, Effects of acid deposition on tree roots, *Ecological Bulletins* **44**, 158–167, 1995.

Pierson, W. R., W. W. Brachaczek, R. A. Gorse, Jr., S. M. Japar, and J. M. Norbeck, Atmospheric acidity measurements on Allegheny Mountain and the origins of ambient acidity in the northeastern United States, *Atmospheric Environment* **233**, 431–459, 1989.

Pitelka, L. F., and D. J. Raynal, Forest decline and acidic deposition, *Ecology* **70**, 2–10, 1989.

Robarge, W. P., and D. W. Johnson, The effects of acidic deposition on forested soils, *Advances in Agronomy* **47**, 1–83, 1992.

Rosengran-Brinck, U., and B. Nihlgård, Effects of nutritional status on the drought resistance in Norway spruce, *Water, Air and Soil Pollution* **85**, 1739–1744, 1995.

Schindler, D. W., A view of NAPAP from north of the border, *Ecological Applications* **2**, 124–130, 1992.

Schulze, E.-D., Air pollution and forest decline in a spruce (*Picea abies*) forest, *Science* **244**, 776–783, 1989.

Schulze, E.-D., O. L. Lange, and R. Oren, eds., *Forest Decline and Air Pollution*, Ecological Studies, Vol. 77, 475 pp, Springer-Verlag, New York, 1989.

Schwartz, S. E., Acid deposition: Unraveling a regional phenomenon, *Science* **243**, 753–763, 1989.

Shannon, J. D., and D. L. Sisterson, Estimation of S and NOx deposition budgets for the United States and Canada, *Water, Air and Soil Pollution* **63**, 211–235, 1992.

Sharpe, W. E., B. R. Swistock, and D. R. DeWalle, A greenhouse study of northern red oak seedling growth on two forest soils at different stages of acidification, *Water, Air and Soil Pollution* **66**, 121–123, 1993.

Shortle, W. C., and E. A. Bondietti, Timing, magnitude, and impact of acidic deposition on sensitive forest sites, *Water, Air and Soil Pollution* **61**, 253–267, 1992.

Shortle, W. C., K. T. Smith, R. Minocha, and W. A. Alexeyev, Similar patterns of change in stemwood calcium concentration in red spruce and Siberian fir, *Journal of Biogeography* **22**, 467–473, 1995.

Sisterson, D. L., et al., Deposition Monitoring: Methods and Results, NAPAP Report 6, Argonne National Laboratory, Argonne, IL, 1990.

Smith, F. B., Emission reductions to meet deposition criteria, *Atmospheric Environment* **26**A, 609–624, 1992.

Smith, W. H., Air pollution and forest damage, *Chemical and Engineering News*, pp. 30–43, Nov. 11, 1991.

Sverdrup, H., P. Warfvinge, and D. Britt, Assessing the potential for forest effects due to soil acidification in Maryland, *Water, Air and Soil Pollution* **87**, 245–265, 1996.

Thomas, F. M., and R. Blank, The effect of excess nitrogen and of insect defoliation on the frost hardiness of bark tissue of adult oaks, *Annals of Science Forestry* **53**, 395–406, 1996.

Thomas, F. M., and U. Kiehne, The nitrogen status of oak stands in northern Germany and its role in oak decline, in L. O. Nilsson, R.F. Hüttl, and U. T. Johansson eds., *Nutrient Uptake and Cycling in Forest Ecosystems*, pp. 671–676, Kluwer Academic Publishers, Netherlands, 1995.

Tiktak, A., and H.J.M. van Grinsven, Review of sixteen forest-soil-atmosphere models, *Ecological Modelling* **83**, 35–53, 1995.

Ulrich, B., Forest ecosystem theory based on material balance, *Ecological Modelling* **63**, 163–183, 1992.

Ulrich, B., The history and possible causes of forest decline in central Europe, with particular attention to the German situation, *Environmental Review* **3**, 262–276, 1995.

Ulrich, B., Nutrient and acid-base budget of central European forest ecosystems, in A. Hutterman, ed., *Effects of Acid Rain on Forest Processes*, Ch. 1, pp. 1–50, Wiley-Liss, New York, 1994.

Walker, R. F., and S. B. McLaughlin, Growth and xylem water potential of white oak and loblolly pine seedlings as affected by simulated acidic rain, *American Midland Naturalist* **129**, 26–34, 1993.

Webb, S. L., and M. G. Glenn, Red spruce decline: A major role for acid deposition, *Ecology* **74**, 2017–2071, 1993.

Williams, M. W., J. S. Baron, N. Caine, R. Sommerfeld, and R. S. Sanford, Jr., Nitrogen saturation in the Rocky Mountains, *Environmental Science and Technology* **30**, 640–646, 1996.

Indications of forest decline

Given the detailed studies of the effects of air pollution on trees, one would expect to find evidence in the forests of decline and increased mortality. That is indeed the case. The references listed here are a sampling of this literature. In the United States, the forest research community has been reluctant to study forest decline in much detail. They will allow that acid ion deposition has killed red spruce in the northeast United States (Eagar and Adams, 1992) and that ozone has killed ponderosa pine in California (Olson et al., 1992). Beyond that, few are willing to state that whatever decline is acknowledged is caused by air pollution. The situation in Europe is much different. The term *"Waldsterben"* or *"forest death"* was coined in Germany in response to the widespread decline in forests noted around the 1980s. Ulrich (1992, 1994) pioneered the study of how acid ion deposition changed soil chemistry. Schulze (1989) and Schulze et al. (1989) showed that acid ion deposition was responsible for much of the decline of the abundant Norway spruce there. While the situation has improved, most likely due to reduced sulfur emissions, an annual survey of forest health is conducted throughout Europe, which is in stark contrast to the situation in the United States,

where the Forest Inventory and Analysis repeat cycle is anywhere from 5 to 22 years!

References

Eagar, C., and M. B. Adams, eds. (1992). *Ecology and Decline of Red Spruce in the Eastern United States*, Ecological Studies, Vol. 96, Springer-Verlag, New York.

Olson, R. K., D. Binkley, and M. Böhm, eds. (1992). *The Response of Western Forests to Air Pollution*, Springer-Verlag, New York.

Schulze, E.-D. (1989). Air pollution and forest decline in a spruce (*Picea abies*) forest, *Science* **244**, 776–783.

Schulze, E.-D, O. L. Lange, and R. Oren, eds. (1989). *Forest Decline and Air Pollution*, Ecological Studies, Vol. 77, Springer-Verlag, New York.

Ulrich, B. (1992). Forest ecosystem theory based on material balance, *Ecological Modeling* **63**, 163–183.

Ulrich, B. (1994). Nutrient and acid-base budget of central European forest ecosystems, in A. Hutterman, ed. *Effects of Acid Rain on Forest Processes*, Ch. 1, pp. 1–50, Wiley-Liss, New York.

Bibliography

Arnolds, E., Decline of ectomycorrhizal fungi in Europe, *Agriculture, Ecosystems and Environment* **35**, 209–244, 1991.

Bechtold, W. A., W. H. Hoffard, and R. L. Anderson, *Forest Health Monitoring in the South*, USDA Forest Service, Southeastern Forest Experiment Station, Gen. Technical Report SE-81, 40 pp, 1992.

Biocca, M., F. H. Tainter, D. A. Starkey, S. W. Oak, and J. G. Williams, The persistence of oak decline in the western North Carolina Nantahala Mountains, *Castanea* **58**, 178–184, 1993.

Bruck, R. I., W. P. Robarge, and A. McDaniel, Forest decline in the boreal montane ecosystems of the southern Appalachian Mountains, *Water, Air and Soil Pollution* **48**, 161–180, 1989.

Byres, D. P., J. D. Johnson, and T. J. Dean, Seasonal response of slash pine (*Pinus elliottii* var. *elliottii* Engelm.) photosynthesis to long-term exposure to ozone and acidic precipitation, *New Phytology* **122**, 91–96, 1992.

European Commission, United Nations Economic Commission for Europe, *Forest Condition in Europe, Results of the 1994 Survey*, 106 pp. plus appendices, 1995, avail. from Dr. M. Lorenz, Federal Research Centre for Forestry and Forest Products, Leuschnerstr. 91, D-21031 Hamburg, Germany.

European Commission, United Nations Economic Commission for Europe, *Forest Condition in Europe, Results of the 1995 Survey*, 128 pp. plus appendices, 1996, avail. from Dr. M. Lorenz, Federal Research Centre for Forestry and Forest Products, Leuschnerstr. 91, D-21031 Hamburg, Germany.

Fox, S., and R. A. Mickler, eds., *Impact of Air Pollutants on Southern Pine Forests*, Ecological Studies, Vol. 118, 513 pp, Springer-Verlag, New York, 1996.

Lambert, N. J., J. Ardö, B. N. Rock, and J. E. Vogelmann, Spectral characterization and regression-based classification of forest damage in Norway spruce stands in the Czech Republic using Landsat Thematic Mapper data, *International Journal of Remote Sensing* **16**, 1261–1287, 1995.

Nilsson, S., and P. Duinker, The extent of forest decline in Europe, *Environment* **29**(9), 4–9, 30–31, 1987.

Oleksyn, J., and K. Przybyl, Oak decline in the Soviet Union—scale and hypothesis, *European Journal of Forest Pathology* **17**, 321–336, 1987.

Oleksyn, J., and P. B. Reich, Pollution, habitat destruction, and biodiversity in Poland, *Conservation Biology* **8**, 943–960, 1994.

Olson, R. K., D. Binkley, and M. Böhm, eds., *The Response of Western Forests to Air Pollution*, Springer-Verlag, New York, 1992.

Powell, D. S., J. L. Faulkner, D. R. Darr, Z. Zhu, and D. W. MacCleery, *Forest Resources of the United States, 1992*, General Technical Report RM-234, 133 pp, USDA Forest Service, Rocky Mountain Forest and Range Experimental Station, Ft. Collins, CO, 1992.

Schütt, P., and E. B. Cowling, *Waldsterben*, a general decline of forests in Central Europe: Symptoms, development, and possible causes, *Plant Disease* **69**, 548–558, 1985.

Wildlife

The books and journals listed here, compiled by Chris Bolgiano in cooperation with Dr. Grant, pertain directly or indirectly to biotic communities and habitats. The impacts of air pollution seriously affect amphibians, fish, soil microorganisms, birds, mammals, and other creatures making their home in Appalachian forests.

Bibliography

Adriano, D. C., and A. H. Johnson, eds. *Acid Precipitation*, Vol. 2, *Biological and Ecological Effects*. (Advances in environmental science series). Springer-Verlag, New York, 1989.

Air pollutants effects on forest ecosystems, The National Acid Precipitation Assessment Program, U.S.D.A. Forest Service, et al. Acid Rain Foundation, 1985.

Baker, Joan P. et al., Biological effects of changes in surface water acid-base chemistry, in *National Acid Precipitation Assessment Program, Acidic Deposition: State of Science and Technology*, Vol. II, NAPAP Report 13, 1990.

Barker, J. R., and D. T. Tingey, eds., *Air Pollution Effects on Biodiversity*, Van Nostrand Reinhold, New York, 1992.

Bartuska, A. M., and S. A. Medlarz, Spruce-fir decline—air pollution related? in *Atmospheric Deposition and Forest Productivity*, proceedings of the 4th regional technical conference at the 65th annual meeting of the Appalachian Society of American Foresters, SAF, Blacksburg, VA, 1986.

Bruck, R. I., W. P. Robarge, and A. McDaniel, Forest decline in the boreal montane ecosystems of the southern Appalachian mountains, *Water, Air and Soil Pollution* **48**, 161–180, 1989.

Bulger, A. J., C. A. Dolloff, B. J. Cosby, K. N. Eshleman, J. R. Webb, and J. N. Galloway, The Shenandoah National Park: Fish in sensitive habitats (SNP: FISH) project, an integrated assessment of fish community responses to stream acidification, *Water, Air and Soil Pollution* **85**, 309–314, 1995.

Chappelka, A. H., S. E. Hildebrand, J. M. Skelly, D. Mangis, and J. R. Renfro, Effects of ambient ozone concentrations on mature eastern hardwood trees growing in Great Smoky Mountains National Park and Shenandoah National Park, paper presented at the 85th annual meeting of the Air and Waste Management Association, 1992.

Chappelka, Arthur et al., Evaluation of ozone injury on foliage of black cherry (*Prunus serotina*) and tall milkweed (*Asclepias exaltata*) in Great Smoky Mountains National Park, unpublished.

Charles, D. F., ed., *Acidic Deposition and Aquatic Ecosystems: Regional Case Studies*, Springer-Verlag, New York, 1991.

Cook, R. B., J. W. Elwood, R. R. Turner, M. A. Bogle, P. J. Mulholland, and A. V. Palumbo, Acid-base chemistry of high-elevation streams in the Great Smoky Mountains, *Water, Air and Soil Pollution* **72**, 331–356, 1994.

Davis, D. D., and J. M. Skelly, Growth response of four species of eastern hardwood seedlings exposed to ozone, acidic precipitation, and sulfur dioxide, *Journal of the Air and Waste Management Association* **42**(3): 309–311, 1992.

Dennis, T. E., S. E. MacAvoy, M. B. Steg, and A. J. Bulger, The association of water chemistry variables and fish condition in streams of Shenandoah National Park (USA), *Water, Air and Soil Pollution* **85**, 365–370, 1995.

Deviney, Frank A., and James R. Webb, St. Mary's River watershed database reference, unpublished, 1993.

Dropping acid in the southern Appalachians, *Trout*, 18–39, Winter 1991.

Dubey, T., S. L. Stephenson, and P. J. Edwards, Effect of pH on the distribution and occurrence of aquatic fungi in six West Virginia mountain streams, *Journal of Environmental Quality* **23**, 1271–1279, 1994.

Eshleman, K. N., L. M. Miller-Marshall, and J. R. Webb, Long-term changes in episodic acidification of streams in Shenandoah National Park, Virginia, USA, *Water, Air and Soil Pollution* **85**, 517–522, 1995.

Fellner, R., and V. Peskova, Effects of industrial pollutants on ectomycorrhizal relationships in temperate forests, *Canadian Journal of Botany* **73**, S1310–S1315, 1995.

Flum, T., and S. C. Nodvin, Factors affecting streamwater chemistry in the Great Smoky Mountains, USA, *Water, Air and Soil Pollution* **85**, 1707–1712, 1995.

Fredericksen, T. S., J. M. Skelly, K. R. Snyder, K. C. Steiner, and T. E. Kolb, Predicting ozone uptake from meteorological and environmental variables, *Journal of the Air and Waste Management Association* **46**, 464–469, 1996.

Fredericksen, T. S., K. C. Steiner, J. M. Skelly, B. J. Joyce, T. E. Kolb, K. B. Kouterick, and J. A. Ferdinand, Diel and seasonal patterns of leaf gas exchange and xylem water potentials of different-sized *Prunus serotina* Ehrh. trees, *Forest Science* **42**(3), 1–7, 1996.

Gill, J. D., ed., *Acidic Depositions: Effects on Wildlife and Habitats*, Technical Review 93-1, The Wildlife Society, Bethesda, MD, 1993.

Godbold, D. L., and A. Huttermann, eds., *Effects of Acid Rain on Forest Processes*, Wiley-Liss, New York, 1994.

Hildebrand, E., J. M. Skelly, and T. S. Fredericksen, Foliar response of ozone-sensitive hardwood tree species from 1991 to 1993 in the Shenandoah National Park, VA, *Canadian Journal of Forest Research* **26**, 658–669, 1996.

Horne, M. T., Metals as potential limiting factors for amphibians which breed in temporary ponds. Dissertation. Pennsylvania State University, University Park, PA, 1994.

Hyer, K. E., J. R. Webb, and K. N. Eshleman, Episodic acidification of three streams in Shenandoah National Park, Virginia, USA, *Water, Air and Soil Pollution* **85**, 523–528, 1995.

Jensen, K. F., and L. S. Dochinger, Response of eastern hardwood species to ozone, sulfur dioxide and acid precipitation, JAPCA **39**, 852–855, 1989.

Johnson, A. H., and S. B. Andersen, Acid rain and soils of the Adirondacks. I. Changes in pH and available calcium, 1930–1984, *Canadian Journal of Forest Research* **24**, 39–45, 1994.

Johnson, A. H., and T. G. Siccama, Acid rain and soils of the Adirondacks. III. Rates of soil acidification in a montane spruce-fir forest at Whiteface Mountain, New York, *Canadian Journal of Forest Research* **24**, 663–669, 1994.

Johnson, D. W., and S. E. Lindberg, eds., *Atmospheric Deposition and Forest Nutrient Cycling: A Synthesis of the Integrated Forest Study*, Springer-Verlag, New York, 1992.

Johnson, D. W., W. T. Swank, and J. M. Vose, Simulated effects of atmospheric sulfur deposition on nutrient cycling in a mixed deciduous forest, *Biogeochemistry* **23**, 169–196, 1993.

Koponen, S., and P. Niemela, Ground-living arthropods along pollution gradient in boreal pine forest, *Entomologica Fennica* **6**, 127–131, 1995.

Koponen, S., and P. Niemela, Ground-living spiders in a polluted pine forest, SW Finland, *Bollettino della Sedute della Accademia Gioenia di Scienze Naturali.* **26**(345), 221–226, 1993.

Leetham, J. W., T. J. McNary, J. L. Dodd, and W. K. Lauenroth, Response of soil nematodes, rotifers and tardigrades to three levels of season-long sulfur dioxide exposures, *Water, Air and Soil Pollution* **17**, 343–356, 1982.

MacAvoy, S. E., and A. J. Bulger, Survival of brook trout (*Salvelinus fontinalis*) embryos and fry in streams of different acid sensitivity in Shenandoah National Park, USA, *Water, Air and Soil Pollution* **85**, 445–450, 1995.

McNulty, S. G., J. D. Aber, and S. D. Newman, Nitrogen saturation in a high elevation New England spruce-fir stand, *Forest Ecology and Management* **84**, 109–121, 1996.

Meier, S., W. P. Robarge, R. I. Bruck, and L. F. Grand, Effects of simulated rain acidity on ectomycorrhizae of red spruce seedlings potted in natural soil, *Environmental Pollution* **59**(4), 315–324, 1989.

"Mountain-dwelling spider may be next protected species," *Asheville Citizen-Times*, sect. B, March 7, 1994.

Neufeld, H. S. et al., Ozone in Great Smoky Mountains National Park: dynamics and effects on plants, in Ronald L. Berglund, ed., *Tropospheric Ozone and the Environment II: Effects, Modeling and Control*, Air and Waste Management Association, Pittsburgh, PA, 1992.

Newman, J. R., and R. K. Schreiber, Effects of acidic deposition and other energy emissions on wildlife: a compendium, *Veterinary and Human Toxicology* **27**(5), 394–401, 1985.

Newman, K., and A. Dolloff, Responses of blacknose dace (*Rhinichthys atratulus*) and brook char (*Salvelinus fontinalis*) to acidified water in a laboratory stream, *Water, Air and Soil Pollution* **85**, 371–376, 1995.

Nodvin, S. C., H. Van Miegroet, S. E. Lindberg, N. S. Nicholas, and D. W. Johnson, Acidic deposition, ecosystem processes, and nitrogen saturation in a high elevation southern Appalachian watershed, *Water, Soil and Air Pollution* **85**, 1647–1652, 1995.

Parsons, J. L. et al., Final report: the diversity of mammals found in declining spruce-fir populations of the southern Appalachian mountains, report to The Nature Conservancy, unpublished.

Read, D. J., Mycorrhizas in ecosystems, *Experientia* **47**, 376–391, 1991.

Ruess, L., P. Sandbach, P. Cudlin, J. Dighton, and A. Crossley, Acid deposition in a spruce forest soil: Effects on nematodes, mycorrhizae and fungal biomass, *Pedobiologia* **40**, 51–66, 1996.

Ruess, L., et al., Influence of experimental acidification on nematodes, bacteria and fungi: Soil microcosms and field experiments, *Zoologische Jahrbuch Syst.* **120**, 189–199, 1993.

Rustad, L. E., and C. S. Cronan, Biogeochemical controls on aluminum chemistry in the O horizon of a red spruce (*Picea rubens* Sarg.) stand in central Maine, USA, *Biogeochemistry* **29**, 107–129, 1995.

Samuelson, L. J., Ozone-exposure responses of black cherry and red maple seedlings, *Environmental and Experimental Botany* **34**(4), 355–362, 1994.

Shubzda, J., S. E. Lindberg, C. T. Garten, and S. C. Nodvin, Elevational trends in the fluxes of sulphur and nitrogen in throughfall in the southern Appalachian mountains: Some surprising results, *Water, Air and Soil Pollution* **85**, 2265–2270, 1995.

Smith, W. H., *Air Pollution and Forests: Interactions between Air Contaminants and Forest Ecosystems*, 2nd ed. (Springer series on environmental management). Springer-Verlag, New York, 1990.

Southern Appalachian assessment: Atmospheric technical report. Prepared by federal and state agencies; coordinated through Southern Appalachian Man and the Biosphere Cooperative. U.S. Forest Service, Atlanta, GA, 1996.

Stanosz, G. R., V. L. Smith, and R. I. Bruck, Effect of ozone on growth of mosses on disturbed forest soil, *Environmental Pollution* **63**, 319–327, 1990.

Straalen, N. M., M. H. S. Kraak, and C. A. G. Denneman, Soil microarthropods as indicators of soil acidification and forest decline in the Veluwe area, The Netherlands, *Pedobiologia* **32**, 47–55, 1988.

U.S. Fish and Wildlife Service, Endangered and threatened wildlife and plants: Spruce-fir moss spider determined to be endangered, *Federal Register* **60**(24), 6968–6974, 1995.

Webb, J. R., B. J. Cosby, J. N. Galloway, and G. M. Hornberger, Acidification of native brook trout streams in Virginia, *Water Resources Research* **25**(6), 1367–1377, 1989.

Webb, J. R., B. J. Cosby, F. A. Deviney Jr., K. N. Eshleman, and J. N. Galloway, Change in the acid-base status of an Appalachian mountain catchment following forest defoliation by the gypsy moth, *Water, Air and Soil Pollution* **85**, 535–540, 1995.

Wheeler, Q. D., and J. V. McHugh, A new southern Appalachian species, *Dasycerus bicolor* (Coleoptera: Staphylinidae: Dasycerinae), from declining endemic fir forests, *The Coleopterists Bulletin* **48**(3), 265–271, 1994.

White, J. J., Woodlice exposed to pollutant gases, *Bulletin of Environmental Contamination Toxicology* **30**, 245–251, 1983.

Wyman, R., Soil acidity and moisture and the distribution of amphibians in five forests of southcentral New York, *Copeia* (2): 394–399, 1988.

A more extensive, comprehensive bibliography, containing 1,700 references and information for contacting corresponding authors is available on a 3.5″ disk in Word-Perfect 5.1 format from the Appalachian Regional Office of the Sierra Club, 69 Franklin St., Annapolis, MD 21401. In addition, readers may wish to consult J. P. Bennett and M. J. Buchen, BIOLEFF: Three databases on air pollution effects on vegetation, *Environ. Pollut.*, **88**, 261–265, 1995. The bibliography is available from Dr. Bennett, University of Wisconsin, Madison, for a nominal fee. It has abstracts of all included listings.

Index

Page numbers in italic refer to illustrations.

213

An Appalachian Tragedy was designed by Tom Suzuki, Tom Suzuki, Inc., Falls Church, Virginia, assisted by Kristin Bernhart, Hea-Ran Cho, Constance D. Dillman, Julienne Lambre and Virginia M. Suzuki. Digital type composition and page layout were produced on Apple Power Macintosh computers. The text type is 11 point Weiss by Neufville S.A., with display type in Gill Sans by Monotype. Italic numbers in the index are set in Perpetua, also by Monotype. Text stock is 130 GSM Burgo R4 Matte, with 50% recycled fiber, of which 15% is postconsumer waste. Color separations, four-color printing and Smythe sewn binding is by Palace Press International, Hong Kong.